"The volume titled *Smart City in India: Urban Laboratory, Paradigm or Trajectory?* authored by Dr Binti Singh and Prof Manoj Parmar is a comprehensive and persuasive presentation of the smart city narrative currently operational in India. It is empirically rich in primary data from second tier smart cities like Lucknow, Jaipur and Varanasi, compiles secondary research from several sources and presents updated data up to the Ease of Living city rankings of 2018. The authors explain that planning and designing of smart cities in India necessitates an inclusive collaboration among residents, designers, and policy-makers. This volume opens new discussions, highlights human and sociological dimensions, and reimaginations in urban design and planning while offering workable solutions and views the smart city mission in India as an opportunity for every selected city to chart its own destiny based on its context."

    – Chetan Vaidya, *Former Director, School of Planning and Architecture (SPA),*
    and National Institute of Urban Affairs (NIUA), New Delhi, India

"*Smart City in India: Urban Laboratory, Paradigm or Trajectory?* is a timely book reflecting on key opportunities in Indian cities. Innovation, sustainability and inclusiveness will have to be major drivers for cities. The authors Dr Binti Singh and Prof Manoj Parmar have compiled this volume based on extensive literature study and empirical cases which I am sure would help academicians and practitioners and people interested in urban affairs in India."

    – Sameer Unhale, *Chief Executive Officer, Thane Smart City Ltd. Thane,*
    Maharashtra, India

"The book is a unique synthesis of a detailed documentation on the concept of smart cities as imagined by the State juxtaposed against the reality and aspirations of its citizens, and an incisive analysis of the 'smart city mission'. The authors have used robust tools for critiquing the project including conversations with stakeholders and multilayered field studies of communities and cities of Lucknow, Varanasi and Jaipur carried out by their students. The book suggests more nuanced ways to reimagine the smart city project. It is a must-read for anyone interested in the current state-of-art in smart city development in India."

    – Alpa Sheth, *Managing Director at VMS Consultants Pvt. Ltd.,*
    Mumbai, India

"I am writing to endorse the upcoming book. In the current scenario of confusion and elusion on the idea of a 'Smart City', *Smart City in India: Urban Laboratory, Paradigm or Trajectory?* by Dr Binti Singh and Manoj Parmar will be able to shed some light on the key aspects of this concept and the various approaches that have been undertaken to implement it in the Indian context. The book illustrates how these approaches to the Smart City idea have been dealt with in the cities of Varanasi, Lucknow and Jaipur. These cities present a complex historic context which makes it interesting to examine how a rather futuristic notion of a 'Smart City' engages with the existing vibrant layer of historicity. To add to this complexity are the realities of life and lifestyles in these cities. It will be therefore interesting to read the critical analysis and challenges of the smart city narrative in the context of urban realities."

– **Navin Piplani**, *Principal Director, INTACH Heritage Academy,*
New Delhi, India

"The collaborated effort of Dr Binti Singh and Prof Manoj Parmar in bringing out this book titled *Smart City in India: Urban Laboratory, Paradigm or Trajectory?* touches upon various issues of smartness itself in the context of Indian cities. Our cities are multi-cultural, multi-aspirational and to bring them into one fold of mono-culture with digito-technological governance will be uncalled for. The book also brings forth the fact that the Special Purpose Vehicle that is to implement the Smart City Plan is not planned or approved or implemented by democratically elected persons but by a set of bureaucrats and international firms determining the destinies of our (smart) cities. This is demeaning [to the] democratic processes of governance. While giving case studies of Lucknow and Varanasi [the] authors have emphasised that 'one-size-fits-all' should not be followed; each city has to formulate its own concept, vision, mission and plan (Smart City Plan/SCP) for a Smart City that is appropriate to its local context, resources and levels of ambition."

– **Sudhir Badami**, *Structural Engineering graduate from IIT Bombay, India;*
he has been carrying out his own to limited extent Research, Advocacy, Planning
and Integrated Design (RAPID) related to urban issues with emphasis on
transportation and air pollution

"In their timely book *Smart City in India: Urban Laboratory, Paradigm or Trajectory?* Manoj Parmar and Binti Singh deliver a first reality check of Narendra Modi's 2015 Smart Cities policy. After a first euphoria for the potential of smart devices in urban planning and management, Parmar and Singh's case studies of recently developed Smart Cities projects in India present a range of challenges, which resonate with the growing public concerns, regarding smart technologies' role in impeding personal privacy, spreading hate speech, manipulating political elections, etc. Parmar and Singh's studies show also how the outsourcing of urban planning and management to international technology giants has weakened democratic planning processes and public accountability, while often failing to deliver robust solutions. In addition, they present how the fixation on Smart City projects contributed to peri-urban development, regional fragmentation and social exclusion. Thus, Parmar and Singh's book reveals three main layers of problems in the implementation of India's Smart Cities Mission and their entanglement with the broader problem of our growing dependency on smart technologies."

– **Hendrik Tieben**, *Associate Professor, School of Architecture, The Chinese*
University of Hong Kong

details, their implications, and their potential impacts on urban planning and management in India."

– **D. Parthasarathy**, *India Value Fund Chair, Department of Humanities and Social Sciences, Indian Institute of Technology (IIT Bombay), Mumbai, India; Convener, Interdisciplinary Program in Climate Studies, IIT Bombay, Mumbai, India*

"The idea of Smart Cities has taken on a mythical status which is not very helpful in thinking about the relationship between technology and urban planning. Through marshalling a range of empirical material on second-tier cities and exploring relationships between residents, private corporations, official bodies and planning ecosystems, this book provides an important overview of actually existing urbanism. It also asks us to remember that Indian cities are sites of great inequalities and urban planning must address this rather than sweep [it] under the carpet."

– **Sanjay Srivastava**, *Professor of Sociology, Institute of Economic Growth, Delhi University Enclave, Delhi, India*

"*Smart City in India: Urban Laboratory, Paradigm or Trajectory?* is a very timely analytical effort. It raises essential questions beyond conventional and rapidly changing terminologies examining what kind of focus, approaches and actions Indian cities need to achieve better livability, economic prosperity, social inclusiveness and sustainability. It rightly brings the discourse to the critical importance of local context tailored development with support of new technologies. I sincerely recommend this book to any urban stakeholder striving to make a difference in their city."

– **Olga Chepelianskaia**, *Founder and Director, UNICITI; Program Manager, Sustainable Cities through Heritage Revival (SEHER Asia)*

"With India on a rapid path to urbanization, the country's Smart City Mission is an important paradigm to understand, given its important role in shaping national urban policy and practice. Smart Cities have been controversial globally, being hailed for their role in improving efficiency and resilience, and critiqued for their impact on social justice and equity. Yet there has been limited scrutiny of this approach in the Indian context. *Smart City in India: Urban Laboratory, Paradigm or Trajectory?* fills an important gap, evaluating the Smart City Mission across the country, and providing an in-depth study in selected cities. Such research is urgently needed to better inform urban policy and practice, towards approaches that are context-specific, inclusive, and people-centric."

– **Harini Nagendra**, *Professor of Sustainability at Azim Premji University, Bangalore, India*

"The Smart City in India confronts the oft-repeated and grandiose stories of how technology is changing urban environments. Combining research from

Lucknow, Varanasi, and Jaipur, along with an analysis of a slum in Mumbai, the book shows the more complicated picture that emerges from close and critical research. The spatial relationships emerging from the insertion of new digital infrastructures into existing urban realities, powered by large-scale government spending and orchestrated to increase further private investment, exacerbate existing social problems. Parmar and Singh bring an important focus to a topic that will elucidate not only the challenges facing India, but facing cities worldwide under the new regimes of neoliberal smartness."

– **Sara Stevens**, *Assistant Professor and Chair of Urban Design, University of British Columbia's School of Architecture and Landscape Architecture in Vancouver, Canada*

SMART CITY IN INDIA

This book is a critical reflection on the Smart City Mission in India. Drawing on ethnographic data from across Indian cities, this volume assesses the transformative possibilities and limitations of the program. It examines the ten core infrastructural elements that make up a city, including water, electricity, waste, mobility, housing, environment, health, and education, and lays down the basic tenets of urban policy in India. The volume underlines the need to recognize liminal spaces and the plans to make the 'smart city' an inclusive one. The authors also look at maintaining a link between the older heritage of a city and the emerging urban space.

This volume will be of great interest to planners, urbanists, and policymakers, as well as scholars and researchers of urban studies and planning, architecture, and sociology and social anthropology.

Binti Singh, Associate Editor, Oxford Urbanists and Faculty, Master's Program in Urban Design and Conservation, KRVIA, Mumbai, India.

Manoj Parmar, Practicing Architect and Dean, Master's Program in Urban Design and Conservation, KRVIA, Mumbai, India.

SMART CITY IN INDIA

Urban Laboratory, Paradigm or Trajectory?

Binti Singh and Manoj Parmar

Routledge
Taylor & Francis Group

LONDON AND NEW YORK

First published 2020
by Routledge
2 Park Square, Milton Park, Abingdon, Oxon OX14 4RN

and by Routledge
52 Vanderbilt Avenue, New York, NY 10017

Routledge is an imprint of the Taylor & Francis Group, an informa business

British Library Cataloguing-in-Publication Data
A catalogue record for this book is available from the British Library

Library of Congress Cataloging-in-Publication Data
Names: Singh, Binti, author. | Parmar, Manoj, author.
Title: Smart city in India : urban laboratory, paradigm or trajectory? /
    Binti Singh, Manoj Parmar.
Description: Abingdon, Oxon ; New York, NY : Routledge, 2020. |
    Includes bibliographical references and index.
Identifiers: LCCN 2019030516 (print) | LCCN 2019030517 (ebook)
Subjects: LCSH: Smart cities—India. | Urban policy—India.
Classification: LCC TD159.4 .S56 2020 (print) | LCC TD159.4 (ebook) |
    DDC 307.760285—dc23
LC record available at https://lccn.loc.gov/2019030516
LC ebook record available at https://lccn.loc.gov/2019030517

ISBN: 978-1-138-60778-1 (hbk)
ISBN: 978-0-367-37404-4 (pbk)
ISBN: 978-0-429-35360-4 (ebk)

Typeset in Bembo
by Apex CoVantage, LLC

This book is dedicated to all stakeholders who are working both individually and collectively to build the urban future of India.

CONTENTS

FIGURES

BOXES

FOREWORD 1

Important books can be important in many different ways. *Smart City in India*, beautifully and rigorously written by Professor Manoj Parmar and Dr. Binti Singh, is important in a way that makes me even more grateful to the authors: it accepts the challenges of the big picture, and it does that competently. Among those challenges, one of the most difficult to deal with is this: when you set yourself out to make sense of a complex phenomenon *as a whole*, you need a point of view on it. In this case, the level of complexity of the phenomenon under scrutiny, contemporary forms of urbanization and urban policies in India, is just overwhelming. The authors' point of view comes out gradually in the reading and shapes up harmoniously through all the threads which reality is made of: in particular, recently introduced public policies and planning ideologies that turn out to reiterate less recent intellectual, political, and economic mechanisms, which they ultimately contribute to further establish in the pulsing body of India.

The authors, significantly an interdisciplinary collaboration between an urban designer and an urban sociologist, look at the Smart City Mission (SCM) in India, introduced in 2015, with a good deal of intellectual freedom, which allows them to get past the thin layer of paint cast over the public discourse by sometimes genuine ideological drivers, as well as clever communication strategies. That results in the construction of *the context* in which the observed phenomenon occurs, first of all its historical context. Far from indulging in criticism at the ideological level, the authors place the SCM into this context in a way that, page after page, makes such criticism unfold by its own force of evidence, on the basis of facts; connections that are evident already and others that are less so become evident because of the way they are presented.

Not just informative, not just enjoyable, this book fully exhibits one quality that heavily contributes to its importance: it is *just*. The reader will feel the moral imperative that sits at the heart of the notion itself of urban design, from the case study part of the research and eventually blasting in the discussion of the informal settlement case in Mumbai. Yes, 'slums' are too densely inhabited, they are poorly serviced and even more poorly maintained. However, they are "a territory of habitation, enterprise and politics [which] opens up new theorizations of Southern cities that do not fit the global cities paradigm as command and control centers, yet are significant in their own right".

It is in the distance between the 'informal settlements' and the 'Smart City' glasses through which the reality of urbanization in India can be looked at that the latter reveals its deep historical nature: one that sits comfortably in the 'urban turn' that caught India as well as many other countries of the Global South in the last three decades or so, one that politically and ideologically qualifies as a direct manifestation of economic liberalization, privatization, and globalization. It is when you look at the informal settlement phenomenon in India that you recognize that the king is naked, and the need to learn from informal settlements is integral with that of seriously addressing their often dramatic hygienic and infrastructural conditions. And they are in fact integral to understanding what *are*, authentically, the booming formal cities for the expanding middle-upper class of India and what *is*, authentically, the climate change challenge that we urban designers must address globally. Now.

Not only a useful, urgent, documented, passionate, well-structured, and intellectually stimulating reading. But an undisputedly *just* one. One that sets a way forward for us all.

Dr. Sergio Porta 17 April 2019

Professor of Urban Design
Department of Architecture
University of Strathclyde
Glasgow, United Kingdom

FOREWORD 2

In this volume titled *Smart City in India: Urban Laboratory, Paradigm or Trajectory?* authors Dr. Binti Singh and Prof. Manoj Parmar have undertaken academic reflection on the very idea of the smart city that seems to be the guiding vision behind many cities, both globally and in India. The volume is based on primary research in the second-tier historic cities of Lucknow, Varanasi, and Jaipur currently implementing smart city projects and also a detailed study of Gazdhar Bandh slum in the megacity of Mumbai. In addition, the authors have compiled innumerable secondary data sources that include detailed information on various cities of India, their current status on smart city projects, and updated data up to the Ease of Living Index released by the Ministry of Housing and Urban Affairs in August 2018.

The authors have not opted for the usual heavy academic criticism, but rather undertake a timely review and reflect on the current urban transformation that India is undergoing and how the Smart City Mission has provided impetus through smart intervention. The authors have cautiously steered from a total dismissal of this intervention but have refreshingly taken a step back to reflect, raise important questions on India's urban realities, and open new conversations on the urban trajectory that 100 smart cities in India have already embarked on and the choices that other cities could opt for.

The authors flag important concerns and challenges related to city governance, human and cultural dimensions, sustainability, informality, and urban design and planning in the current narrative. With several examples across cities of India and smart city projects and plans currently operational, they argue that there is time for course correction, factoring in India's commitment to Goal 11 of the SDGs, quintessential components of Indian cities that may have been missed and crucial sociological and human concerns that could pave the way forward for the smart cities of tomorrow. Rather than despair, the authors choose hope for

India's urban future and see the Smart City Mission as an opportunity that has opened up new pathways that cities in India could work on, capitalizing on their own strengths to chart their own destiny.

I sincerely believe that this book will serve as a rich resource for urban researchers, officials, professionals, and urban managers.

Dr. Ramnath Sonawane, Chief Executive Officer,
Nagpur Smart and Sustainable City Development Corporation Ltd.,
Nagpur, India

ABBREVIATIONS

ABD	Area-Based Development
AI	Artificial Intelligence
AMRUT	Atal Mission for Rejuvenation and Urban Transformation
ANPR	Automatic Number Plate Recognition
ANVP	Atal Nagar Vikas Pradhikaran
APEDA	Agricultural and Processes Food Products Export Development Authority
ASI	Archaeological Survey of India
BHU	Banaras Hindu University
BOT	Built–Operate–Transfer
BRTS	Bus Rapid Transit System
CBO	Community-Based Organization
CCTV	Closed-Circuit Television
CEO	Chief Executive Officer
CSR	Corporate Social Responsibility
DPRs	Detail Project Reports
ELU	Existing Land Use
FY	Financial Year
GDP	Gross Domestic Product
GIFT	Gujarat International Finance Tec-City
GPS	Global Positioning System
HLRN	Housing and Land Rights Network
IAS	Indian Administrative Service
ICCC	Integrated Command and Control Centre
INTACH	Indian National Trust for Art and Cultural Heritage
IOT	Internet of Things

JNNURM	Jawaharlal Nehru National Urban Renewal Mission
JSCL	Jaipur Smart City Limited
LAP	Local Area Plan
LED	Light Emitting Diode
LIDAR	Light Detection and Ranging
MCGM	Municipal Authority of Greater Mumbai
MHADA	Maharashtra Housing and Area Development Authority
MMRDA	Maharashtra Metropolitan Regional Development Authority
MNCs	Multinational Companies
MOHUA	Ministry of Housing and Urban Affairs
MOUD	Ministry of Urban Development
MRTP	Maharashtra Regional and Town Planning Act, 1966
NDA	National Democratic Alliance
NDMC	New Delhi Municipal Council
NGO	Nongovernmental Organization
NIFT	National Institute of Fashion Technology
NIMZ	National Investment and Manufacturing Zones
ODF	Open Defecation Free
ODOP	One District One Product
PMAY	Pradhan Mantri Awas Yojana
PMC	Project Management Consultant
PPP	Public Private Partnership
PWD	Public Works Department
RAY	Rajiv Awas Yojana
SASA	Safe and Secure Ahmedabad
SBM	Swachh Bharat Mission
SCC	Smart City Centre
SCM	Smart City Mission
SCP	Smart City Plan
SDG	Sustainable Development Goals
SEZ	Special Economic Zone
SIB	Slum Improvement Board
SLNA	State-Level Nodal Agency
SPV	Special-Purpose Vehicle
SRA	Slum Rehabilitation Authority
SRS	Slum Resettlement Scheme
SWM	Solid Waste Management
TCPO	Town and Country Planning Organization
TPS	Town Plan Schemes
TRPs	Television Rating Points
TV	Television
ULB	Urban Local Body
UNESCO	United Nations Educational, Scientific and Cultural Organization

UP	Uttar Pradesh
UPA	United Progressive Alliance
UT	Union Territory
VDA	Varanasi Development Authority
VSCL	Varanasi Smart City Limited

1

INTRODUCTION

A newspaper article in a Sunday daily carried this news: "Smart locks, lights turn tools of domestic abuse... Internet connected home devices are being used to harass, monitor and control". The article reported how abusers – using apps on their smart phones, which are connected to Internet-enabled devices – would remotely control objects in the home, sometimes to watch and listen, other times to scare or show power. Some of tech's biggest companies make smart home products. For victims and emergency responders alike, such experiences of abuse, violence and crime are often aggravated by a lack of knowledge about how smart technology works and, most importantly, how much power the other person has over these devices, how to legally deal with abusive behavior and overall concerns of safety (Bowles, 2018).

The recent controversy over vulnerabilities related to the disclosure of the *Adhar* number, invasion of privacy, social media hub, and draft bill on data protection and e-commerce opened up new debates and raised questions on how smart India is with the Internet, social media, and digital technologies. How advanced are our digital technologies? Do we have the technological infrastructure to support huge swathes of data floating in the public domain? Are new technologies invading our private lives? Are we jeopardizing our safety by sharing too much data?

The word 'smart' entered the urban lexicon when the government of India announced its massive Smart City Mission (SCM) in 2015. Soon after, national-level summits and conferences were abuzz with best practices and role models about what a smart city in India should be. As participants in many of these events, we could witness the huge business opportunities that the very idea of a smart city brings. Along came new terms like digital technologies, smart technologies, artificial intelligence (AI), robotics, and the Internet of Things (IOT), machine learning, and blockchain. The range of private participants selling a plethora of e-based solutions to pressing urban issues like waste management, public toilets, traffic, and transport is the most noticeable feature in these summits and conferences. People across the table talked, argued, and debated about smart solutions to urban challenges.

In this volume, we do not intend to answer the question: What is a smart city? Rather we leave that question open for multiple answers. That is the reason the title of this volume ends with a question mark. Is the smart city a new paradigm, is it a laboratory, or is it a new trajectory? We think it is a bit of all of this. The idea of a smart city has opened up a new arena of opportunities that has translated cities as laboratories for new experiments. There is no universally accepted definition of a smart city. 'Smart', 'intelligent', or 'digital' are varied ways of denoting the current concept of smart cities that has become common parlance in urban policy discourse worldwide. As Vito Albino (2015) notes, the term was first used in the 1990s when the use of newly emerging information and communication technologies (ICTs) for urban infrastructures was emphasized. The California Institute for Smart Communities was among the first to focus on how communities could become smart and how a city could be designed to implement information technologies (Alawadhi et al., 2012), later critiqued by the Center of Governance at the University of Ottawa as being a too technically oriented concept. Engineers, information technology (IT) professionals, and marketing professionals continue to read and interpret smart cities from the vantage point of their respective discipline and training. A social science and cultural understanding are starkly missing.

A smart city in India will have a different connotation than elsewhere. Within India, too, there is no one way of defining a smart city.

The questions we pose in this opening chapter are:

1   Is there a pattern that can be discerned from the various smart experiments that have translated our cities as labs?
2   Is the SCM in India connected to the challenges posed by the current trends of urbanization?
3   What are the challenges to smartness?
4   What are the alternative pathways and reimagining that could inform the smart city discourse currently underway?

These questions form the bedrock of this volume and are explored in subsequent chapters, drawing from empirical evidence from ongoing smart city projects and case studies. While exploring these questions, the trajectory of urban development processes in India is traced from independence in 1947, discussed in Section 1. This overview of urbanization in India helps situate urban missions like the Jawaharlal Nehru National Urban Reforms Mission (JNNURM) in 2005 and trace it to the current smart cities paradigm launched in 2015 (for details see MoUD, 2015) discussed in Section 2. Section 3 discusses the significance of the study, and Section 4 presents an overview of the chapters in this volume.

Section 1: urban planning and development in India

In post-independent India, urbanization unfolded in the form of industrial townships, satellite towns, and state capitals (Datta, 2012; Dossal, 2010; Sivaramakrishnan, 1978; Kalia, 1994, 1999, 2004; Parry and Strümpel, 2008). Significant urban planning initiatives at the national level were formalized encompassing economic and social content. The urban development planning system as per Urban Development Plans Formulation and Implementation (UDPFI) guidelines consists of set of inter-related plans, namely a Perspective Plan, which is a long term plan with socioeconomic components; a Development Plan is conceived within the framework of a Perspective Plan with a mid-range time frame for the development of urban areas affecting spatial-economic development; and Annual Plans are conceived within the framework of a Development Plan implemented within one fiscal year. From the point of view of physical planning, for the first time, several cities witnessed modern planned development. This meant acquiring land; laying out roads, pipelines, sewers, and drains; and providing electricity, schools, and health and sanitation facilities. In many such resettled colonies, one-or two-room houses were also allotted. This period lasted nearly for a decade, until it was felt that municipal corporations should be set up to manage urban affairs. In 1959, the New Delhi Municipal Corporation Act was passed to set up a corporation. Another parallel development saw the setting up of the Delhi Development Authority (DDA), under the Delhi Development Act 1962 to acquire lands, execute planned development on the basis of master plans, and disburse/allocate plots for multifarious purposes. This model of having two separate legally constituted agencies to deal with urban issues in a city, though imperfect, caught on with the imagination of the time, and the trend still continues in many states, even after the enactment of the 74th Constitutional Amendment Act (CAA) in 1992. Development authorities, whose main purpose was to develop new serviced land and create housing stock, operated in unique ways. They acquired large tracts of land in the name of creating a pool (to avoid speculation), planning for the long term while holding it for decades and releasing the land gradually. Although their modern town planning model was premised on the principles of a garden city movement that promoted healthy living through open green areas and egalitarian distribution of resources, systematic zoning of work areas, residential units, and road planning, while executing it, these authorities failed miserably. While lagging to track the actual demand, they created a legacy of an urban pattern that is highly unsustainable and socially exclusive. The so-called planned cities are marred with a wide separation of work places and residential districts, increase in travel distances, dependency on roads for travel, relegating natural features like hill crops and rivers to the backyard, prioritizing high-income and middle-income housing, keeping original villages out of planned development, leaving undeveloped large parcels of vacant land within the city, and cookie-cutter mass housing models with little cultural affinity. In effect, not only are the planned cities highly unlivable for the vast populace, these also promote economic inefficiencies, location disadvantages, and spatial inequities that eventually serve as a breeding ground for social disparities to flourish.

Some of the major milestones in the planned development of towns and cities in India include:

- Enactment of the Delhi Development Act 1957, leading to establishment of the DDA, followed by establishment of about 300 development authorities for as many cities.
- Launching of national schemes such as Integrated Development of Small and Medium Towns (IDSMT) Scheme in the Sixth Five-Year Plan (1980–85), intended to address critical development needs of small and medium towns.
- Publication of India's first urbanization policy in 1988 by the National Commission on Urbanization (NCU) chaired by Charles Correa. This document was the first to point out the inevitable leading role of cities in driving forward India's economy and the necessity of integrating the spatial and economic development of its urban centers.
- Enactment of the 73rd and 74th Constitutional Amendments in 1992 known as the Panchayati Raj Act and Nagarpalika Act, respectively. These empowered elected representatives of districts or urban local bodies (ULBs) to undertake economic and spatial planned development of villages, towns, and cities. But because land is a state subject, only some states adopted the acts, resulting in slowdowns on the implementation side.
- In 2005 the government of India, led by the United Progressive Alliance (UPA), launched the JNNURM, which was the first initiative of its kind in terms of the scale of investment of USD 20 billion over a period of seven years. Sixty-five cities were selected under this initiative.
- In June 2015, the government of India, led by the National Democratic Alliance (NDA), initiated the SCM. Its objective is to improve the conditions of 100 cities within five years, with an approved investment of USD 15 billion.

(www.athenainfonomics.in/2017/11/06/urban-planning-india
and UDPFI GUIDELINES)

Section 2: the urban turn in India

A sense of desperation and restlessness on the part of the newly elected NDA in May 2014 provided the much-needed impetus for the launch of the SCM in India in 2015. The NDA came to power with a thumping majority and riding high on the faith bestowed by middle-class, urban, educated Indians mostly living and working in urban areas. The new government entered office with the promise of good governance, growth, and development. Much of this growth was about the rapidly urbanizing India. Hence, a national-level mission to capture this growth was imminent. India does not live in villages anymore. This is a claim based on statistics. For the first time since independence, the absolute increase in population is more in urban areas than in rural areas (Census of India, 2011). With a total urban population of 377 million in India, urbanization increased from 27.81% in 2001 to 31.16% in 2011 (MoUD, 2011). The variation may seem marginal, but urban India is actually adding almost four times the Australian population every decade. The urban population is increasing at 2.76% annual exponential growth rate, while the rural population is increasing at 1.15%. Moreover, the absolute increase in population is more in urban areas than in rural areas, largely on account of net rural urban classification and migration (56%) against natural increase (44%). As per an assessment by the Town and Country Planning Organisation (TCPO), there are 7,935 towns (4,031 statutory towns and 3,894 census towns) in India (TCPO, 2012). In 2001, the figure was 5,161 towns (3,799 statutory towns and 1,362 census towns).[1] The statutory towns have increased by 6.37% and the census towns by 185%, signifying that a number of rural areas have attained urban characteristics and been designated as census towns. Out of 7,935 towns in India, 468 are Class I (population more than 0.1 million) and 53 are million-plus cities. Almost four out of every five Class I towns have a population of 0.1 to 0.5 million (TCPO, 2012). The average size of towns and cities in India has grown from 33,624 in 1961 to about 61,159 in 2011, thus clearly indicating that urbanization in India is evident both in geographical spread and sheer volume (TCPO, 2012). It has been observed that the growth in big metros is gradually stabilizing, while the newer and smaller cities are growing faster. It took nearly 40 years (1971–2011) for India's urban population to rise to 270 million; in the future it may take half the time to add the same number. According to various estimates, by 2030, India's urban population will be 590 million (McKinsey Global Institute, 2010) to 600 million (Ministry of Urban Development (MoUD, 2011) – that is, about 40% of the total and break-even with the rural population by 2039.

Clearly, the urban turn in India has happened. The spate of urban policies from 2015 onwards, namely, the Atal Mission for Rejuvenation and Urban Transformation (AMRUT), Swachh Bharat Mission (SBM), Digital India, and SCM, have for the first time subjected cities in India to rigorous attempts at transformation. These patterns of transformation, however, were set in motion by a series of interventions post-1990 brought about by adopting the policy of economic liberalization, privatization, and globalization (collectively known by the acronym LPG), decentralization and good governance discourse, and flagship urban programs like the JNNURM (www.jnnurm.nic.in) in 2005.

The urban turn could be more precisely termed as the neoliberal turn in India's urbanization with attendant urbanisms. The impacts are especially visible in the ways in which urban policies and practices have shaped up since then. First, the cumulative effects of LPG led to planned urban development brought about with the entry of private players in large-scale infrastructure development, like highways, flyovers, expressways, and townships; greenfield urban development like industrial parks and townships; Special Economic Zones (SEZs); and National Investment Manufacturing Zones (NIMZs). Second, urban governance has altered significantly in India with the entry of private players in the provision of basic services. This is witnessed in new modes of revenue generation, like the introduction of pay and use services (toilets, garbage collection), capital market borrowing, and increased charges to cope with rising infrastructure costs, as well as new institutional arrangements like public–private partnerships, built–operate–transfer (BOT), community-based projects, and the institution of special-purpose vehicles (SPVs) to undertake urban governance functions. The changes in urban governance are also witnessed in the ability of ULBs to raise funds on the bond market or enter into loan agreements for infrastructure development, environmental improvement, and administrative reform with foreign funders (Singh, 2014; Zerah, 2009; Chaplin, 2007; Benjamin, 2000). Third, urbanization and urbanism in India are inspired by global symbols, models, and aspirations, like those of world-class cities, global cities, and now smart cities. These influences are currently underway, and cities in India have opportunities for course correction if they so desire.

Section 3: significance of the study

This study is based on secondary literature sources and primary data mainly drawn from second-tier cities across India, as these are the major labs for smart city experiments. Second-tier cities of cultural significance like Lucknow, cities of religious significance like Varanasi, and those of historical significance like Jaipur are case studies in this volume. Besides, the slum community of Gazdhar Bandh in Mumbai also serves as a case study to examine questions of informality and how these could be incorporated in community-based planning models. Like other Indians, we intend our cities to be smart, modern, well connected, and global. As academics, we are wary of the lopsided vision, misplaced priorities, urban design methods, and their larger implications on the questions of urban equity and sustainability. Globally urban discourse is being shaped by the New Urban Agenda agreed recently to in Habitat III in 2016 and Goal 11 of the Sustainable Development Goals (SDGs) and the general discussion around sustainable cities. This global discourse collectively acknowledges urban inequities and calls for more inclusive, safe, resilient, and sustainable cities. In its policy, India has shown commitment to the goal of inclusive urbanization with schemes like the Urban Basic Service Program, Indira Awas Yojna, Valmiki Ambedkar Aawas Yojna, Rajiv Awas Yojana, and Pradhan Mantri Awas Yojna that have aimed to facilitate essential services and shelter the urban poor. Talking to government officials, it became abundantly clear that there are attempts to converge these various schemes with the smart cities narrative. India is also committed to global goals like the SDGs and the New Urban Agenda adopted during the Habitat III Conference in Quito in October 2016 guided by the principle of leave no one behind – all firmly committed to providing equal access for all, to physical and social infrastructure and basic services, and to adequate and affordable housing. The SBM, AMRUT, SCM, and Housing for All by 2022 introduced by the government of India in 2015 emphasize the actualization of these very objectives on the ground.

The smart city is the new paradigm driving urban policy and governance in India, as in other parts of the world. The smart city as an idea is open to myriad interpretations. It is with this understanding that the government of India (GoI) has allowed each of the 100 smart cities (so far enlisted) to chart out its own path towards becoming a smart city based on its own specific context. Research on smart cities in India is rare, and the existing literature does not present a comprehensive understanding based on a wide range of empirical cases (Sood and Kennedy, 2016; Kennedy, 2007; Kennedy and Zérah, 2008; Ren and Weinstein, 2013). This volume seeks to fill the gap in the existing literature based on a detailed study of the SCM in India currently operational, presents critical reflections, and suggests an alternative framework based on detailed case studies. The vision and plan of smart cities currently operational in India is an eventual process tied to procedures, sanctions, funding, and implementation engaging various agencies and institutions. These institutions overlap the terrain of the state and market and include government, public, semi-public agencies, private companies, civil society organizations, and citizens at large. Technologies, especially digital technologies, form the core of this narrative. This together with the rampant privatization of essential services and private capital–driven urbanization processes, render the urban story of India rather fuzzy and uncertain. This volume, based on recent examples from cities across India, flags missing points in the current narrative and reflects and reimagines the current narrative. The best practices and models provide a basket of choices. The question is how we tailor them to suit our needs and contexts. As we bring out the best practices and discuss the various experiments in cities across India and based on our detailed case studies of Lucknow, Varanasi, and Jaipur, we critically argue for fundamental aspects that have been grossly overlooked (or simply ignored) in the overenthusiasm of creating smart cities in India. In a bid to come up with a common language to break down the silos of professional thinking and practice, we suggest a reimagining of the current narrative, a rethinking of urban design and planning practices with workable operational frameworks for different urban contexts.

Section 4: overview of chapters

Chapter 2 is a detailed description of the SCM in India launched in 2015 along with a discussion of other urban programs that were launched at the same time. These include ARMRUT, SBM, Digital India, HRIDAY, and Housing for All by 2022. The chapter touches upon key highlights of the SCM in India, namely, driving competitive federalism through a series of performance benchmarks, awards and indices; introduction of new institutions like SPVs; emphasis on private participation (mainly corporates, tech giants, and startups); innovative technologies; and interfaces between citizen and government for efficient urban management. The chapter also discusses various smart city initiatives currently underway in cities across India.

Chapters 3 and 4 draw the attention of the reader to second-tier cities of India like Jaipur, Madurai, Lucknow, and Varanasi. These cities also happen to be historic cities currently subjected to pressures and pulls of uneven urbanization, experiments, and plans. These often do not address fundamental challenges and ignore the organic character of these cities, adding layers of infrastructure that are disconnected from the core, resulting in spatial divisions and social disconnect between people, places, and occupations and eventual loss of urban tissue. Chapter 3 examines these essential features of Indian urbanism and how they are missed in the smart city narrative based on the empirical cases of smart city plans currently operational in the cities of Lucknow and Varanasi. Chapter 4 extends this discussion with a detailed spatial analysis of the historic city of Jaipur and the importance of urban design therein. Chapter 5 extends the discussion of Indian urbanism to the challenges of informality. Specifically, it discusses how informality has been disregarded in urban planning practices in India and in the SCM narrative guiding current urban discourse in India. Based on the case of Gazdhar Bandh, an informal settlement in a commercial precinct of Mumbai, the chapter argues how incremental housing and community-driven design and planning at the micro level could help build inclusive, resilient, safe, and sustainable cities. This chapter also emphasizes the significant role that urban design can play in the growth and development of cities and suggests an operational framework. Chapter 6 presents the concluding remarks by revisiting the questions asked at the outset. It critically analyses the SCM narrative by flagging key missing points, social and environmental vulnerabilities, the question of citizen rights, safety, and privacy and highlights the growing challenges of the current urbanization trends that SCM is silent on.

Note

1 The Census of India (2011) considers two types of towns (urban centers), namely (a) statutory towns: all places with a municipality, corporation, cantonment board or notified town area committee, etc., so declared by state law; and (b) census towns: places which satisfy the following demographic criteria: (i) a minimum population of 5,000, (ii) at least 75% of the male working population engaged in nonagricultural pursuits, and (iii) a density of population of at least 400 persons per km^2.

References

Alawadhi, S. et al. (2012). Building understanding of smart city initiatives. In H. J. Scholl, M. Janssen, M. A. Wimmer, C. E. Moe, and L. S. Flak (eds.), *Electronic Government: EGOV 2012: Lecture Notes in Computer Science* (Vol. 7443). Berlin, Heidelberg: Springer. https://doi.org/10.1007/978-3-642-33489-4_4

Albino, V., U. Berardi and R. M. Dangelico (2015). Smart cities: definitions, dimensions, performance, and initiatives. *Journal of Urban Technology*, 22(1), 3–21. doi:10.1080/10 630732.2014.942092

Benjamin, S. (2000). Governance, economic settings and poverty in Bangalore. *Environment and Urbanization*, 12(1), 11–49.

Bowles, N. (2018). Smart locks, lights turn tools of domestic abuse: times trends. *The Times of India*, Lucknow, Tuesday 26 June, p. 13.

Census of India (2011). *Provisional Population Totals-2011, Paper – II* (Vol. II). New Delhi: Census of India, p. 1.

Chaplin, S. (2007). Partnerships of hope: new ways of providing sanitation services in urban India. In A. Shaw (ed.), *Indian Cities in Transition*. New Delhi: Orient Longman, pp. 83–103.

Datta, P. (2012). *Planning the City: Urbanization and Reform in Calcutta, c 1800-c 1940*. New Delhi: Tulika Books.

Dossal, M. (2010). *Theatre of Conflict, City of Hope: Mumbai 1660 to Present Times*. New Delhi: Oxford University Press.

Kalia, R. (1994). *Bhubaneswar: From a Temple Town to a Capital City*. Carbondale and Edwardsville: SIU Press.

Kalia, R. (1999). *Chandigarh: The Making of an Indian City*. New Delhi: Oxford University Press.

Kalia, R. (2004). *Gandhinagar: Building National Identity in Postcolonial India*. Columbia, SC: University of South Carolina Press.

Kennedy, L. (2007). Regional industrial policies driving peri-urban dynamics in Hyderabad, India. *Cities*, 24(2), 95–109.

Kennedy, L. and M.-H. Zérah (2008). The shift to city-centric growth strategies: perspectives from Hyderabad and Mumbai. *Economic & Political Weekly*, 43(39), 110–17.

Mckinsey Global Institute (2010). *India's Urban Awakening: Building Inclusive Cities Sustaining Economic Growth*. New Delhi: Mckinsey Global Institute, pp. 13–35.

Ministry of Urban Development (MoUD) (2011). *India's Urban Demographic Transition: The 2011 Census Results-Provisional*. New Delhi: JNNURM Directorate and National Institute of Urban Affairs, pp. 2–4.

Ministry of Urban Development (MoUD) (2015). *Smart Cities: Mission Statement & Guidelines*. New Delhi: Ministry of Urban Development, Government of India.

Parry, J. and C. Strümpel (2008). On the desecration of Nehru's "temples": Bhilai and Rourkela compared. *Economic & Political Weekly*, 43(19), 47–57.

Ren, X. and L. Weinstein (2013). Urban governance, mega-projects and scalar transformations in China and India. In T. R. Samara, S. He, and G. Chen (eds.), *Locating Right to the City in the Global South*. London and New York: Routledge, pp. 107–26.

Singh, B. (2014). Urban governance in contemporary India. *Contemporary India*, 4, 89–111.

Sivaramakrishnan, K. C. (1978). *New Towns in India, a Report on a Study of Selected New Towns in Eastern Region*. Calcutta: Indian Institute of Management.

Sood, A. and L. Kennedy (2016). Greenfield development as tabula rasa rescaling, speculation and governance on India's urban frontier. *Economic & Political Weekly*, LI(17), 41–49, 23 April.

TCPO (2012). *Data Highlights (Urban) Based on Census of India*. New Delhi: Town & Country Planning Organisation, pp. 1–19.

Zerah, M. H. (2009). Participatory governance in urban management and the shifting geometry of power in Mumbai. *Development and Change*, 40(5), 853–77.

Online source

www.athenainfonomics.in/2017/11/06/urban-planning-india accessed on 7 September 2018 and UDPFI GUIDELINES.

2

SMART CITY MISSION IN INDIA

This chapter is a description of the Smart City Mission (SCM) in India, its convergence with other urban programs and policies launched around the same time, the institutional framework created for implementation of the SCM in India, and examples from cities across India. The SCM covers 100 cities, and its duration is five years (FY2015–16 to FY2019–20). The SCM lists ten core infrastructures in the urban economy that include water, electricity, waste, mobility, housing, environment, health, and education. The SCM also charts out over 20 technology-supported smart solutions. In addition, the SCM offers unique features of comprehensive development in smart cities that include promoting mixed land use in area-based developments, housing, and inclusiveness, creating walkable localities, preserving and developing open spaces, promoting a variety of transport options, making governance citizen-friendly and cost-effective, giving an identity to the city, and applying smart solutions to infrastructure and services.

The strategic components of area-based development in the SCM are city improvement (retrofitting), city renewal (redevelopment), and city extension (greenfield development) in addition to a pan-city initiative in which smart solutions are applied covering larger parts of the city. The government of India (GoI) does not prescribe any particular model to be adopted by the smart cities. The approach is not one-size-fits-all, as each city has to formulate its own concept, vision, mission, and plan (Smart City Plan [SCP]) for a smart city that is appropriate to its local context, resources, and levels of ambition. The criteria for selecting smart cities is based on nomination by states/union territories (UT) and competitive selection. The 100 smart cities have been distributed among the states and UTs on the basis of an equitable criteria. The formula gives equal weight (50:50) to the urban population of the state/UT and the number of statutory towns in the state/UT. Based on this formula, each state/UT will therefore have a certain number of potential smart cities, with each state/UT having at least one.

In 2018 the Ministry of Housing and Urban Affairs in New Delhi launched Local Area Plan (LAP) and Town Plan Schemes (TPS) for 25 smart cities to accelerate area-based infrastructure and planned urban expansion with a central assistance of Rs 50 crore for 25 states for LAP and TPS. The assistance will be released in three installations: 20% with the submission of a preliminary proposal and 40% during submission of a final plan. To enable planning for developing infrastructure in brownfield and greenfield areas, respectively, the LAP and TPS were formulated under the Atal Mission for Rejuvenation and Urban Transformation (AMRUT). This exercise will take a period of one year, wherein the preliminary proposal is for two months and the draft plan includes ten months. For this, the Town and Country Planning Organization (TCPO) will aid the state nodal agency (MoHU, 2018).

The Smart City paradigm, along with other urban policies like AMRUT and Heritage Development and Augmentation Yojana (HRIDAY), has laid out the future pathways of urban India discussed in detail in Section 1. Section 2 describes the institutional framework put in place for the implementation of SCPs and projects across the 100 selected smart cities in India. This section highlights the emphasis of the SCM on citizen engagement, providing an environment for private enterprises and startups that would provide digital solutions to pressing issues of urban management. The Ministry of Housing and Urban Affairs also launched smart cities fellowship and internship programs in 2018 to enable youth participation in different aspects of urban planning and governance. The ministry has envisaged engaging 30 young graduates, postgraduates, and PhD holders in fields of urban planning, finance, social sector, urban design, environmental issues, information and technology, urban mobility, and engineering. Section 3 collates various initiatives currently underway in India that are often touted as best practices, role models, and success stories. Section 4 concludes this chapter with critical questions that are examined in detail in subsequent chapters with the help of detailed case studies of SCPs currently operational in cities like Lucknow, Varanasi, and Jaipur.

Section 1: convergence of SCM with other urban programs

This section describes the plethora of urban schemes and programs launched since 2015 that work in convergence with the SCM (Table 2.1).

Section 2: institutional framework

The implementation of the SCM at the city level will be carried out by a special-purpose vehicle (SPV) created for the purpose. The SPV will plan, appraise,

TABLE 2.1 Urban programs working in convergence with the Smart City Mission

S. No.	Scheme	Date of launch	Scheme details	Geographic focus areas
1	Smart Cities	25 June 2015	Urban renewal and retrofitting program with the mission to develop 100 cities across the country making them citizen-friendly and sustainable	India state wise and city wise
2	AMRUT	25 June 2015	Ensuring water supply, sewerage, and septage management; storm water drainage; urban transport; and availability of green and open spaces, as well as reform management and support, and capacity building	India state wise and city wise
3	Swachh Bharat Mission	2 October 2014	Making urban India free from open defecation and achieving 100% scientific management of municipal solid waste in 4,041 statutory towns in the country	State wise, city wise, and ward wise
4	HRIDAY	21 January 2015	Focus on holistic development of heritage cities	National level, India city level, city wise
5	National Urban Transport Policy	2006	Bus Rapid Transit System (BRIS), urban transit infrastructure or financing of metro rail projects.	Urban
6	North Eastern Region Urban Development Program (NERUDP)	2009	Covering priority urban services viz. (a) water supply, (b) sewerage and sanitation, and (c) solid waste management besides capacity building, institutional and financial reforms	India and state wise
7	Scheme for Satellite Towns around seven megacities	2009	Use of information and communication technologies (ICT) to enhance the access and delivery of government services to benefit citizens, employees, and management of urban local bodies	State wise
8	Pradhan Mantri Awas Yojana (Urban)	2015	In situ rehabilitation of existing slum dwellers using land as a resource through private participation, credit-linked subsidy, affordable housing in partnership, and subsidy for beneficiary-led individual house construction/enhancement	State wise
9	Make inn India	2014	To encourage companies to manufacture their products in India	India
10	Digital India	2014	To ensure that government services are made available to citizens electronically by improved online infrastructure and by increasing Internet connectivity, or by making the country digitally empowered in the field of technology	India and state wise

Source: Authors.

approve, release funds, implement, manage, operate, monitor, and evaluate the smart city development projects. Each smart city will have an SPV, which will be headed by a full-time chief executive officer (CEO) belonging to the Indian Administrative Services and have nominees of central government, state government and urban local bodies (ULBs) on its board. The states/ULBs shall ensure that (a) a dedicated and substantial revenue stream is made available to the SPV so as to make it self-sustainable and could evolve its own credit worthiness for raising additional resources from the market and (b) government contributions for a smart city is used only to create an infrastructure that has public benefit outcomes. The execution of projects may be done through joint ventures, subsidiaries, public–private partnerships (PPP), turnkey contracts, suitably dovetailed with revenue streams (MoUD, 2015). The ensuing discussion enlists and describes the roles of multiple stakeholders in the implementation of SCM in India:

1 The SPV will be a nodal agency in implementing this program. It will plan, appraise, approve, release funds, implement, manage, operate, monitor, and evaluate the smart city development projects

The SPV may appoint project management consultants (PMCs) for designing, developing, managing, and implementing area-based projects. SPVs may take assistance from any of the empaneled consulting firms in the list prepared by the MoUD and the handholding agencies. For the procurement of goods and services, transparent and fair procedures as prescribed under the state/ULB financial rules may be followed. Model frameworks as developed by the MoUD may also be used for smart city projects.

The key functions and responsibilities of the SPV are to:

a   Approve and sanction the projects, including their technical appraisal.
b   Execute the smart city proposal with complete operational freedom.
c   Take measures to comply with the requirements of the MoUD with respect to the implementation of the smart cities program.
d   Mobilize resources within timelines and take measures necessary for the mobilization of resources.
e   Approve and act upon the reports of a third-party review and monitoring agency.
f   Overview capacity building activities.
g   Develop and benefit from interlinkages of academic institutions and organizations.
h   Ensure timely completion of projects according to set timelines.
i   Undertake review of activities of the mission, including the budget, implementation of projects, and preparation of SCP and coordination with other missions/schemes and the activities of various ministries.
j   Monitor and review quality control–related matters and act upon issues arising thereof.

k Incorporate joint ventures and subsidiaries and enter into PPPs as may be required for the implementation of the smart cities program.

l Enter into contracts, partnerships, and service delivery arrangements as may be required for the implementation of the SCM.

m Determine and collect user charges as authorized by the ULB.

n Collect taxes, surcharges, etc., as authorized by the ULB monitoring of the mission.

2 City-level monitoring

A Smart City Advisory Forum will be established at the city level for all 100 smart cities to advise and enable collaboration among various stakeholders and will include the district collector, member of parliament, member of legislative assembly, mayor, chief executive officer of SPV, local youths, technical experts, and at least one member from the area who is a:

President/secretary representing the registered Residents Welfare Association

Member of a registered Taxpayers Association/Rate Payers Association

President/secretary of a slum-level federation

Member of a nongovernmental organization (NGO) or Mahila Mandali/ Chamber of Commerce/Youth Associations

The CEO of the SPV will be the convener of the Smart City Advisory Forum.

3 Municipal authorities

Municipal authorities, or *Nagar Nigam*, are the main supporting pillars of the SCM that operate at the city level. Their roles and functions are enumerated in the Twelfth Schedule (Article 243-W) which lists 18 functions that could be devolved to municipalities by the state government indicating an overlapping.[1] The Constitution of India describes India as a union of states. The center legislates on its subjects (List I), the states have exclusive power in certain areas (List II), share power with the center in some fields (List III), and control the administrative machinery at the lower levels.

4 Private companies

Private companies are major players in the implementation of smart city projects. Most of this private space is occupied by global technology giants like Cisco, IBM, and Bosch, that are showing keen interest in participating in the setting up of smart city centers or integrated command and control systems. According to reports, big private companies like HP and Siemens are working to set up such a center in Bhopal, while Bosch, Cisco, Efkon, and Rolta are participating in the development of a smart city center in Varanasi. Honeywell is doing the same in Bhubaneshwar, and Schneider, Cisco, and HP are setting up a center in Naya Raipur. Leading Indian firms, including Larsen and Toubro, Shapoorji Pallonji Group, Bharat Electronics Ltd., and Tech Mahindra, are also participating with global technology giants to set up smart city centers, which are key to the mission. Each of the 100 cities selected under the government's SCM will get Rs 500 crore to carry out the projects. Tenders have been called for 55 cities for setting up such centers, which would entail an investment of Rs 5,300 crore, while works worth Rs 2950 crore have started in 23 cities. Smart centers in eight cities – Ahmedabad, Vadodara, Surat, Pune, Nagpur, Rajkot, Visakhapatnam, and Kakinada – have become operational. These cities are monitoring various services at the center, which include solid waste collection, smart streetlights, and a transit management system. These centers also offer a city-wide surveillance system to enable the administration and police department keep a watch on sensitive areas, such as major traffic junctions and tourist places (Smart City Mission: Tech giants showing interest in setting up smart city centres April 29, 2018).

5 Smart city center

Every selected smart city in India will have what is known as a smart city center (SCC), commonly understood as an integrated command and control center. However, based on the way in which it is imagined and designed, the SCC will play a much larger role in the urban story of India. In an influential article titled 'How the smart cities project is transforming India's urban governance,' in *Hindustan Times*, 5 July 2018, Hardeep S. Puri, Union minister of state (Independent Charge) for Housing and Urban Affairs, explains the vision behind an SCC. He writes: "The SCC functions as a city's nervous system where digital technologies are integrated with social, physical, and environmental aspects of the city, to enable centralized monitoring and decision making. In the SCC architecture, Internet of Things (IoT) devices such as sensors, Global Positioning System (GPS) equipment and cameras located at the front-end (trash bins, vehicles, streets, and poles) collect and transmit data through a communication network to a central facility. Applications then convert the data and information received into insights, which further facilitates a decision support system. The SCC thus enables real-time monitoring and expeditious incident response management in city operations." The SCC, though cost intensive, is an urban innovation bringing together technology, architecture, and governance in a way that makes urban living convenient in many ways. The use of IoT and artificial intelligence (AI) in SCCs address quality of services, safety and resilience, inclusiveness in city operations, faster emergency response management, and environmental sustainability. Results are already visible. For instance, the article cites examples from Pune, Rajkot and Kakinada, Ahmedabad, Bhopal, and Vishakhapatnam.

SCCs will help generate new enterprises, thereby increasing employment opportunities because the SCM focuses on innovative projects and startups for better provision of services to urban residents. In addition, the coming together of technology companies and engineering and construction firms (mostly Indian firms) in the development of SCCs will help improve urban livelihoods. Urban governance is envisioned to be improved with the efficacy of SCCs, which focuses on integration of a wide range of services and convergence with other city projects. The minister pins hope on civil society, NGOs, academic institutions, industry, and citizens for harnessing these opportunities and proactively improving the urban landscape of India.

6 Citizens and communities

Keeping in mind the participatory approaches in current public policy, citizen participation plays a significant role in the SCM paradigm. Digital technologies are said to play the major role in creating this interface between government and citizens. The use of social media alongside digital technologies and their varied applications has received high priority under the SCM like never before. We already know about the implications of social media and digital technologies in all spheres of social existence. For instance, recent research has highlighted the significance of social media and new modes of communication on social movements (Kadoda and Hale, 2015; Harindranath and Khorana, 2014; Sakr, 2013), civic engagement and neighborhood associations (Johnson and Halegoua, 2015), digital neighborhoods (Anselin and Williams, 2015), social capital (Kingsley and Townsend, 2006), election outcomes (Barclay et al., 2015), and political beliefs (Wang, 2014).

The SCM narrative stands on the pillar of smart digital technologies and their applications. Each municipal authority in India has heavily invested its resources for digitalization of its records and training of in-house staff for such functions. More often than not, they have to depend on private firms to provide them with support services and to develop such applications. For instance, the SCP of Lucknow aspires to reposition the city as the heritage and cultural capital of the country. In order to translate this vision into reality, the SCP lays out detailed ways in which government would engage citizens and heavily depends on social media for the same. A wide variety of electronic platforms, including (a) MyGov.in (discussion forums, poll, essay competition, and vision competition); (b) Twitter; (c) Facebook; (d) Google forms; (e) Smart City Lucknow.com; (f) WhatsApp; (g) direct e-mailing; and (f) Instagram and other online activities, as well as light emitting diode (LED) vans and advertisements in media (both print and electronic) have been listed that will bolster the SCM in Lucknow. The municipal authority of Lucknow incorporated citizens' suggestions through an organization called the Lucknow Management Association while preparing the draft SCP for the city in 2014–15 (lmc, 2016).

Lucknow's SCP is based on the following vision:

> Lucknow Smart City aspires to leverage its culture and heritage by invest-
> ing in inclusive and transformative solutions that enhance the quality of
> life for its citizens.
>
> *(Executive Summary Smart City Proposal -*
> *Fast Track Lucknow, 2016)*

Section 3: smart city initiatives across India

This section highlights smart city initiatives across India since 2015. In Rajkot, the crime rate has reduced by 18% over the past two quarters as of April 2018. There is also an improvement in traffic *challans* issuance, indicating behavioral change. Monitoring of cleaning work through closed-circuit television (CCTV) cameras has led to reduction in instances of littering, urination in public, and nighttime burning of garbage.

In Kakinada, environment sensors have been deployed for automatic weather monitoring, air quality monitoring, and lightning detection.

Pune has installed flood sensors at key points around the city, which feed data to the SCC, enabling a timely warning and response mechanism. Emergency callboxes have been installed at 120 locations to contact the nearest police station with just the press of a button.

In Ahmedabad, free Wi-Fi on BRTS corridors has increased ridership by 20,000 in March 2018, compared to February 2018.

In Vishakhapatnam, CCTV and GPS-enabled buses are being tracked online.

Bhopal has seen a rise in its property tax collections and is also able to track its transport services online (How the smart cities project is transforming India's urban governance, *Hindustan Times*, 5 July 2018).

Ludhiana is selected as one of the 20 Light House Cities under the SCM and is the largest business and trade hub for north India and Asia's largest hub for bicycle manufacturing and hosiery. By 2025 Ludhiana aspires to be the most bicycle-friendly city in India that will transform itself from being a car-dependent city to a bicycle and pedestrian priority city. To that end, the SPV is holding competitions like Make Your City Smart and inviting citizens, students, technical experts, teachers, and others to design streets and junctions and parks. The design components include streetscape enhancement for a safe and walkable environment, as well as façade improvement and locating power cables underground. The streetscape toolkit includes landscape, hardscape with walkways and plazas, street furniture, lighting, parking rearrangements, garbage bins, public toilets, bicycle stands, signage, and wayfinding elements. The areas chosen for the competition are Redesign of Municipal Park (mygov, 2019) and Redesign of Ghumar Mandi road (details available in www.mygov.in/sites/default/files/mygov_146658539933847684.pdf;) (mygov, 2019).

Raipur, Atal Nagar (formerly known as Naya Raipur) and Bilaspur are the emerging smart cities of India through various intelligent experiments that are often claimed as the best India has seen in recent years.

BOX 2.1: EMERGING SMART CITIES IN INDIA: RAIPUR, ATAL NAGAR, AND BILASPUR

The smart initiatives in Raipur include planning for redevelopment of the old Jawahar Bazaar, whose structurally weak walls posed a danger to the life and property of hundreds of shopkeepers and thousands of daily visitors. All stakeholders were called in and presented with different plans prepared by the authorities. Interestingly, all 170 shopkeepers in the area had no objection to the project and willingly settled, as they were given the freedom of allocating their own shops within the legal framework. It is one of the biggest market redevelopment projects undertaken by any of the smart cities in the country claimed by reports.

The *5AM Army* campaign brought together the citizens of Raipur to address the unsanitary practice of open defecation. It comprises an army of civilians who start work at 5 a.m. every morning. Such had been the group's effectiveness that the end of 2017 saw Raipur officially declared ODF. The *Neki Ki Deewar* campaign was unfurled recently as a campaign for anonymous gifting and the dignified receiving of charity. The *Selfie-with-Plant* campaign brought people together to plant a tree in the right season and geo-tag it on the Mor Raipur app. Within a month more than 8,000 plants were geo-tagged. This pool of crowd sourced information allows not just the monitoring of funds better but helps technology use to preserve nature, according to officials. Atal Nagar has made headlines for its major eco-development projects that mandate every building in the city to be equipped with rainwater harvesting, solar energy, and Internet connectivity. An innovative utility corridor that would enable services such as water supply, sewerage, telecom, and electricity – all efficiently located underground – is another facet. About 27% of its land has been earmarked for afforestation and greening initiatives, and Atal Nagar bears the rare distinction of being a 'zero discharge' city with decentralized sewage treatment and has advanced water management projects, including wastewater recycling, smart meters, rainwater harvesting, and green infrastructure, to keep storm water overflow at bay. Atal Nagar has all its streets illuminated with network controlled, energy-efficient light-emitting diode (LED) lights along with cycling tracks that have been laid across the city to encourage a nonmotorized commuting system. And for those who love walking, *Ekatm Path*, a 2.2-km-long boulevard, has been laid down. *Jungle*

Safari, a manmade forest safari right in the cityscape precincts, is claimed to be Asia's largest. Digital utility services, like paying one's taxes, bills, commute passes, and municipal services to a traceable grievance redressal system that ensures transparency through online accountability of all public offices, are in the pipeline. One can avail themselves of all these services by linking their registered mobile numbers to this system. Rajat Kumar, CEO of Atal Nagar Vikas Pradhikaran (ANVP), says: "Inclusiveness, making the city green, transit and job-oriented development as well as making the city accessible for all sections of society are areas we are trying to focus on after having extensively worked on infrastructure, bringing smart elements in and getting smart technology that would monitor how the city functions. This is the next stage that we are trying to move towards." Bilaspur is amongst the nine cities in Chhattisgarh that are receiving a major infrastructural facelift with focus on areas such as water supply, sewerage and septage management, stormwater drains, pedestrian comforts, nonmotorized and public transport facilities, parking space, green spaces, and park and recreation centers. It is also part of the center's AMRUT mission. The whole city is divided into 502 grids, where each grid is manned by proportionate personnel and machinery that have evidently resulted in optimization of existing manpower, thereby reducing operations and maintenance (O&M) costs and drastically improving service delivery. A prominent project spearheaded in the city has been to switch from a conventional overhead electricity supply system to an underground one that envisions providing around-the-clock power supply across the city. For ensuring a 24 × 7 water supply, municipal authorities are incorporating advanced measures, like a redesigned stormwater system, hydrological information system, and a mandatory shift to rainwater harvesting for eliminating dependence on groundwater. Through smart metering and supervisory control and data acquisition (SCADA) systems, Bilaspur intends to provide an interminable electricity and water supply for its citizens. In addition, the city is addressing its waste management issues by augmenting collections points across its precincts for managing sewerage/septage, e-waste, hazardous waste, and plastic waste. An integrated solid waste management plant, the first in Chhattisgarh, was inaugurated in Bilaspur. The facility has a capacity of 200 tons per day and ensures that the roughly 2 lakh kilos of waste generated by the city on a daily basis is turned into utility products through recycling. As for sustainable practices, solar plants and rooftop solar panels are being incorporated to meet energy requirements. The roads in Bilaspur have also switched to smart LED illumination and are 100% solar powered. Various initiatives are also being proposed, with the future goal of making every citizen in Bilaspur skilled by 2030, starting with government schools offering skill development (*Sangawari*) for students in the evening under the PPP model. Schools are also in the process of being equipped with Atal Tinkering Labs, a program fronted by NITI Aayog, under which seven locations have been identified by concerned authorities in Bilaspur that would be linked to research and innovation councils and forums. Bilaspur has a smart 'City-Jan' card for all its citizens that bridges the gap between the people and administration by integrating various e-governance and public services powered by a digital wallet – all under one single platform. One can make use of the smart bus and parking facilities, recharging stations, and *Rent-a-Cycle* scheme using this card across the city. An online public feedback system is also in place that allows people to share ideas or suggestions, as well as file grievances. Labor markets or *Chowdis* are being upgraded to a formal platform by integrating e-skill and digital employment exchange portals.

Source: Lekshmi, P. S. (2018).

Section 4: SCM narrative: where are cities in India heading?

Based on the earlier discussion, this section attempts to highlight crucial points in the new narrative of urban development and governance. These include competitive federalism, privatization, municipal administration, administrative efficiency versus questions of equity, sustainability, significance of urban design and planning, and informality. These are further critically examined in subsequent chapters based on primary empirical data and case studies. The rest of this section highlights these pointers with recent examples linking them to the larger implications on urban planning, development, and governance.

First, the idea of competitive federalism has caught on like never before, with city and state governments aggressively competing for projects, investments, rankings, and awards. The India Smart Cities Award was launched on 25 June 2017 with an objective to reward cities, projects, and innovative ideas promoting sustainable development in cities. The Housing and Urban Affairs (HUA) Ministry, New Delhi, regularly makes official announcements of winners and losers. The project awards are given to the most innovative and successful projects in seven categories. On 1 April 2018, the India Smart Cities Award was given to the following cities in various categories:

Surat has been awarded for showcasing great momentum in the implementation of projects in the categories of urban environment, transport and mobility, and sustainable integrated development under the SCM.

Bhopal was recognized for its Integrated Command and Control Centre (ICCC) and Ahmedabad for its Safe and Secure Ahmedabad (SASA) Project were selected in the 'Innovative Idea' category for their transformative approach towards sustainable integrated development.

Nine smart cities, including the New Delhi Municipal Council (NDMC), bagged project awards for innovative and successful projects in seven categories, according to the official announcement of the ministry in 2018.

Under the 'Social Aspects' category, NDMC and Jabalpur (in Madhya Pradesh) received the award for implementation of a smart classrooms project, Visakhapatnam was selected for its smart campus project, and Pune for a lighthouse project in which underprivileged youths of the city get a chance to explore possibilities for enhancing their skills and pursuing a meaningful career.

In the 'Urban Environment' category, Bhopal, Pune, and Coimbatore received the award for a public bike sharing project, and Jabalpur was selected for its waste-to energy plant project.

Bhopal and Jaipur got awards in the 'Culture and Economy' category, Ahmedabad and Surat in the 'Transport and Mobility' category, Ahmedabad under the 'Water and Sanitation' category, and Pune under the 'Governance' and 'Built Environment' categories (Surat bags award for 'great momentum' in implementation of Smart City projects the Housing and Urban Affairs (HUA) Ministry said today, 2019).

Competitive federalism is gaining impetus in the whole design of the SCM. The ranking of cities, performance benchmarks to procure funds from central government, and selection criteria have resulted in intense competition among ULBs and state government departments. The annual rankings of cities on a sanitation index, livable cities ranking, open defecation free (ODF), and other criteria are just a few. For instance, the Swachh Survekshan is a pan-Indian exercise to assess cleanliness in urban India. In 2018 as part of this exercise, as many as 4,203 cities were surveyed from 4 January to 10 March 2018. Indore is India's cleanest city, followed by Bhopal (ranked second in two consecutive years), followed by Chandigarh in third place. The *Swach Survekshan* surveyed 4,203 cities in 2018 as compared to only 434 cities surveyed in 2017. Ghaziabad in Uttar Pradesh was declared the fastest-moving big city, while Jharkhand has been declared the best-performing state, followed by Maharashtra, in the *Swachh Survekshan* 2018. The criteria of assessment are based on data submitted by civic bodies on cleanliness and sanitation and feedback from citizens with regard to ODF progress, collection, transportation, and processing of solid waste.

Second, successful implementation of projects depends on the engagement of citizens. Hardeep Singh Puri, Union Minister for HUA, tweeted that the big winning cities have actually turned the *Swachhata*/cleanliness mission into a people's movement, or *Jan Andolan*. Citizen engagement with local government resonates with similar initiatives in the megacities of India and global trends that could be read within the broader framework of decentralized governance and participatory planning strategies (see Singh, 2013).

Third, successful implementation of programs also depends on cultural and social practices, many of which are rural in character. The rapid urban transition of India has yet to keep pace with age-old practices. Films like *Toilet Ek Prem Katha* have brilliantly portrayed the intricacies of the problem rooted in traditions and cultural practices. The main challenge for the successful implementation of this program is not just building an adequate number of toilets. The question is how many people will use them.

Fourth, successful implementation of projects requires coordination and cooperation of other important government departments. For instance, the municipal authority is unable to address the problem of ODF on its own. It requires the coordination and cooperation of other important government departments, like the railways. In a city like Lucknow, the Lucknow Municipal Corporation is trying hard to stop people from using vacant land within railway boundaries for defecating. As a result, Lucknow lost out on its Swachh Bharat Rankings in 2018, and is yet to be declared ODF. The ODF parameter carried 150 marks in the Swachh Bharat Mission (SBM) 2018 rankings. And Lucknow scored 0 out of 150. If the city can declare itself ODF and this is found true during spot checking, the center will give 75 marks. Cities stand to lose in terms of negative marking from the center if claims are found to be false.

Fifth, performance benchmarks appear as a smart strategy to improve the efficiency of municipal services. The annual ranking of cities is a great way to keep city municipal departments on their toes for better performance. Indian cities have long suffered from the administrative apathy of municipal authorities. Municipal authorities get away with poor performance in constitutionally mandated functions like solid waste management, road maintenance, water, and sanitation services. Citizens interviewed in this study see the performance indicators of municipal authorities as a welcome move. Indian cities were supposed to be ODF by 2019, but many cities are lagging far behind. The cities that have been poor performers include Lucknow, the capital city of one of India's most populous states, Uttar Pradesh. Lucknow was ranked 269th in 2017 and in 2018 it secured 115th place in city rankings. Poor sanitation, failure to ensure door-to-door garbage collection, improper solid waste management, and lack of citizen participation have been cited as the reasons for this dismal performance. Girish Mishra, corporator of the Sardar Patel Nagar award in Lucknow, notes: "The ranking shows that Lucknow municipal corporation officials are not ready to work hard to keep the city clean. They failed to overcome last year's shortcomings to improve the rankings. Finishing at 115th is indeed shameful" (Srivastava, 2018).

Sixth, urban governance is increasingly becoming the handiwork of private players like tech giants and multinational companies (MNCs). Economic liberalization in 1991, with the attendant needs to attract foreign investment, especially for physical infrastructure in urban centers, brought about deregulation of the economy with direct impact on urban governance. These impacts are especially visible in the ways in which urban policies and practices have shaped up since then. The entry of private players in large-scale infrastructure development includes highways, flyovers, expressways, townships, greenfield urban development like industrial parks and townships, SEZs, NIMZs, and now smart cities; in the provision of basic services; new modes of revenue generation like the introduction of pay and use services (toilets, garbage collection), capital market borrowing, and increased water charges to cope with rising infrastructure costs; new institutional arrangements like PPPs, divestment, community-based projects, and SPVs; and the ability of ULBs to raise funds on the bond market or enter into loan agreements for infrastructure development, environmental improvement, and administrative reform with foreign funders (Singh, 2014; Zerah, 2009; Chaplin, 2007; Benjamin, 2000). In the wake of the introduction of the economic reforms and decentralized governance heavily championed by international agencies like the World Bank, planners and policymakers in India have made a strong case to make parastatal agencies and ULBs depend increasingly on their internal resources and institutional finance, with the objective of bringing in efficiency and accountability. SCM accelerates the privatization, further opening up crucial urban municipal services to private capital. However, questions of equity, regulation, and justice remain.

To conclude, the plethora of random initiatives across cities and the multitudes of private players in the implementation of such initiatives have rendered cities laboratories for experiments. It has only been four years since the launch of the SCM in India, so the timeline is too short for a full-blown critical analysis or to arrive at any conclusive overstatement. There is time for course correction, but only if misplaced priories are corrected and a holistic vision is restored. For one, the SCM fails to provide a holistic integrated paradigm or a trajectory for future pathways. The SCM stands on projects that are too short term and sporadic in nature. There are several gaps in the implementation of SCM across the cities of India. In many cities, projects have not moved beyond the pilot stage or are stuck halfway. Proposals to create smart city subcommittees, including one on gender, have not taken off. The SCM narrative is also silent on crucial questions of Indian urbanism, like rights and entitlements of informal settlements and in providing adequate standards to guide project implementation, including for housing, water, sanitation, health, and environmental sustainability.

The SCM has left the fate of the urban future of India in the hands of private players and their business interests. Urban governance is fuzzier and lacks regulation. It is also silent on how to improve the existing urban governance framework constitutionally mandated in the 74th CAA, 1992, and existing provisions like improving municipal capabilities, representation of municipal councilors, and strengthening of participatory forums like ward committees. The smart solutions that are offered under the smart city projects are already mentioned as important functions to be performed by urban local bodies in the 12th schedule of the Constitution of India. Many state governments have already passed conformity legislation in their respective states and thereby have recognized an elaborate role for ULBs to play in the governance of their urban spaces.

SCM, just like its predecessor JNNURM, empowers the state-level government agencies. The State-Level Nodal Agency (SLNA) under JNNURM and the SPV under SCM are state-level executive bodies headed by centrally appointed Indian Administrative Service (IAS) officers that may infringe on the functional jurisdiction of the democratically and constitutionally elected ULBs and duplicate functions.

The larger questions of good urban design, urban planning, sustainability, and inclusion are missing in this narrative. A report prepared by the Housing and Land Rights Network (HLRN), New Delhi, notes that the SCM model creates small area-based smart enclaves. These area-based development zones cover less than 5% of the geographic domain of many of the proposed smart cities. The scheme could perpetuate existing biases and discrimination in national planning processes by aiming to affect the lives of only 8% of India's population, the report says. Beyond the vision and framework, actual implementation of even the projects that have been proposed has been slow, the report notes, citing a recent parliamentary standing committee report. In its March 2018 report, the standing committee had noted that of all urban schemes, spending on SCM had been the lowest. Only 8% of the total identified projects under the mission have been completed in three years (Sreevatsan, 2018).

In the next chapter we discuss SCM along with a spate of other recently launched urban policies in the state of Uttar Pradesh. The chapter highlights SCM in the cities of Varanasi and Lucknow that serve as cases for detailed examination of the questions raised in this chapter.

Note

1 The 18 additional functions are:

> 1. Urban planning, including town planning; 2. Regulation of land use and construction of buildings; 3. Planning for economic and social development; 4. Roads and bridges; 5. Water supply for domestic, industrial, and commercial purposes; 6. Public health, sanitation, conservancy, and solid waste management; 7. Fire services; 8. Urban forestry, protection of the environment, and promotion of ecological aspects; 9. Safeguarding the interests of weaker sections of society, including the handicapped; 10. Slum improvement and upgradation; 11. Urban poverty alleviation; 12. Provision of urban amenities and facilities such as parks, gardens, and playgrounds; 13. Promotion of cultural, educational, and aesthetic aspects; 14. Burials and burial grounds; cremations, cremation grounds, and electric crematoriums; 15. Cattle pounds: prevention of cruelty to animals; 16. Vital statistics, including registration of births and deaths; 17. Public amenities, including street lighting, parking lots, bus stops, and public conveniences; and 18. Regulation of slaughterhouses and tanneries.
>
> *(Article 243-W, Constitution of India)*

References

Anselin, L. and S. Williams (2015). Digital neighborhoods. *Journal of Urbanism, International Research on Placemaking and Urban Sustainability.* doi:10.1080/17549175.2015.1080752

Barclay, F. P., C. Pichandy, A. Venkat and S. Sudhakaran (2015). India 2014: Facebook "like" as a predictor of election outcomes. *Asian Journal of Political Science*, 23(2), 134–60. doi:10.1080/02185377.2015.1020319

Benjamin, S. (2000). Governance, economic settings and poverty in Bangalore. *Environment and Urbanization*, 12(1), 11–49.

Chaplin, S. (2007). Partnerships of hope: new ways of providing sanitation services in urban India. In A. Shaw (ed.), *Indian Cities in Transition*. New Delhi: Orient Longman, pp. 83–103.

Draft Smart City Plan (2015). Lucknow Municipal Authority.

Executive summary smart city proposal - fast track Lucknow. mc.up.nic.in/pdf/Executive Summary.pdf accessed on 17 September 2016.

Harindranath, R. and S. Khorana (2014). Civil society movements and the "twittering classes" in the post-colony: an Indian case study. *South Asia: Journal of South Asian Studies*, 37(1), 60–71. doi:10.1080/00856401.2012.744285

How the smart cities project is transforming India's urban governance. *Hindustan Times*, 5 July 2018. www.hindustantimes.com/analysis/india-s-urban-landscape-is-changing/story-4Q2gmRJhiGwRrdtv9ToTMN.html accessed on 10 September 2018.

Johnson, B. J. and G. R. Halegoua (2015). Can social media save a neighborhood organization? *Planning Practice & Research*, 30(3), 248–69. doi:10.1080/02697459.2015.1051319

Kadoda, G. and S. Hale (2015). Contemporary youth movements and the role of social media in Sudan. *Canadian Journal of African Studies/ Revue Canadienne des études Africaines*, 49(1), 215–36. http://dx.doi.org/10.1080/00083968.2014.953556 accessed on 06 July 2018.

Kingsley, J. Y. and M. Townsend (2006). "Dig in" to social capital: community gardens as mechanisms for growing urban social connectedness. *Urban Policy and Research*, 24(4), 525–37. doi:10.1080/08111140601035200

Lekshmi, P. S. (2018). Atal Nagar, Raipur & Bilaspur: Chhattisgarh's Smart Cities Are Redefining India. www.thebetterindia.com/160196/news-chhattisgarh-raipur-bilaspur-atal-nagar-smart-city/, 25 September, accessed on 10 June 2019.

Ministry of Urban Development (MoUD) (2015). *Smart Cities: Mission Statement & Guidelines*. New Delhi: Ministry of Urban Development, Government of India.

Sakr, L. S. (2013). A digital humanities approach: text, the internet, and the Egyptian uprising. *Middle East Critique*, 22(3), 247–63. doi:10.1080/19436149.2013.822241

Singh, B. (2013). Governance, citizens and new civil society in contemporary urban India. *ORF Issue Brief No. 54*, June. http://orfonline.org/cms/export/orfonline/modules/issuebrief/attachments/Issuebrief54_1371713087707.pdf1–12 accessed on 06 July 2018.

Singh, B. (2014). Urban governance in contemporary India. *Contemporary India*, 4, 89–111.

Smart city mission: tech giants showing interest in setting up smart city centres (2018). 29 April. https://m.economictimes.com/news/economy/infrastructure/smart-city-mission-tech-giants-showing-interest-in-setting-up-smart-city-centres-says-official/articleshow/63959537.cms accessed on 10 September 2018.

Surat bags award for "great momentum" in implementation of smart city projects the Housing and Urban Affairs (HUA) Ministry (2018). 20 June. New Delhi: PTI. www.financialexpress.com/infrastructure/surat-bags-award-for-great-momentum-in-implementation-of-smart-city-projects/1214148/ accessed on 10 June 2019.

Sreevatsan, A. (2018). Smart cities mission is too project-based and lacks integrated vision: report. Friday 22 June. www.livemint.com/Politics/sMVEQUQKo83bsG9C-2De7RP/Smart-Cities-Mission-is-too-projectbased-and-lacks-integrat.html accessed on 10 June 2019.

Srivastava, A. (2018). 115th sanitation ranking shows city still stinks. *Hindustan Times*, Lucknow edition, 25 June.

Wang, S. (2014). Internet exposure and political beliefs among educated youth in China. *Journal of Contemporary China*, 23(90), 1133–51. doi:10.1080/10670564.2014.898903 http://lmc.up.nic.in/pdf/SCP_Lucknow.pdf accessed on 17 September 2016.

Zerah, M. H. (2009). Participatory governance in urban management and the shifting geometry of power in Mumbai. *Development and Change*, 40(5), 853–77.

Online sources

http://amrut.gov.in/writereaddata/Programme%20Management_City%20Level.pdf accessed on 10 June 2019.

http://amrut.gov.in/writereaddata/Programme%20Management_National%20Level.pdf accessed on 10 June 2019.

http://amrut.gov.in/writereaddata/Programme%20Management_State%20Level.pdf accessed on 10 June 2019.

http://digitalindia.gov.in/node/170 accessed on 10 June 2019.

www.hindustantimes.com/analysis/india-s-urban-landscape-is-changing/story-4Q2gmRJhiGwRrdtv9ToTMN.html accessed on 10 June 2019.

http://hridayindia.in/institutional-framework-and-governance-structure/ accessed on 10 June 2019.

www.mygov.in/sites/default/files/mygov_146658524733847684.pdf accessed on 10 June 2019.

www.mygov.in/sites/default/files/mygov_146658539933847684.pdf accessed on 10 June 2019.

www.mygov.in/task/make-your-city-smart-ludhiana/ accessed on 10 June 2019.

http://mohua.gov.in/cms/pradhan-mantri-awas-yojana.php accessed on 10 June 2019.

http://mohua.gov.in/upload/uploadfiles/files/List_empanelled_consultants011.pdf accessed on 10 June 2019.

http://mohua.gov.in/upload/uploadfiles/files/UIDSST-Primers.pdf accessed on 10 June 2019.

http://smartcity.eletsonline.com/mohua-launched-lap-and-tps-for-25-smart-cities/ accessed on 20 August 2018.

http://smartcities.gov.in/content/innerpage/city-level.php accessed on 10 June 2019.

http://smartcities.gov.in/content/innerpage/national-level.php accessed on 10 June 2019.

http://smartcities.gov.in/content/innerpage/state-level.php accessed on 10 June 2019.

http://smartcities.gov.in/upload/uploadfiles/files/SPVs.pdf accessed on 10 June 2019.

www.swachhbharaturban.in/sbm/home/#/ContactDetails accessed on 10 June 2019.

www.swachhbharaturban.in/sbm/home/#/ULBContactDetails accessed on 10 June 2019.

3

PACKING HISTORY AND CULTURE WITH SMARTNESS

The cases of Lucknow and Varanasi

Urban heritage and culture have always been neglected areas in the cities of India. Indian cities are embedded in history, with a rich cultural heritage spanning over centuries. Successive empires and dynasties have added to the complexities of the urban landscape that are still reflected in the built environment and the strong presence of local traditions. Many are worth revisiting, learning from, and, above all, conserved. For instance, the *Vastu Purusha Mandala* principles of planning of early Indian cities (a geometric pattern representing the cosmos, often associated with Jaipur); the dense, irregular urban grid framework of medieval cities; and cultural practices, customs, rituals, and traditions are recognized as essential components of each city's identity, like the Ganga Arti in Varanasi, the *Kumbh Mela* in Allahabad and Nasik, the *PhoolWalon Ki Sair* Festival in Delhi, and *Ganjing* in Lucknow or *Vasant Utsav* in Shantiniketan. Some cities in India have been proactive in reviving some of these cultural practices. The Hunnarshala Foundation is actively involved in the revitalization of traditional building techniques in Bhuj, Gujarat, following the earthquake in 2001. Cities like Varanasi and Jaipur have joined the UNESCO Creative Cities Network. UNESCO declared Ahmedabad as a heritage city in 2017. On 30 June 2018 in the UNESCO World Heritage Committee meeting in Bahrain, Mumbai's Victorian and Art Deco Ensembles in the heritage precincts of Fort and Marine Drive were inscribed as UNESCO World Heritage Site.

In this chapter we examine how the essential features of old historic cities are being worked into the smart city narrative. Lucknow and Varanasi are two of the ten cities selected in the Smart City Mission (SCM) in Uttar Pradesh (UP). The other cities from UP selected in the SCM are Allahabad, Aligarh, Kanpur, Jhansi, Agra, Bareilly, Moradabad, and Saharanpur. The cases of Lucknow and Varanasi are chosen as case studies for several reasons. First, both are important cities in the state of UP located in the north of India. Second, both cities have rich histories and are places of cultural and religious significance. Third, both cities have been part of many policies on heritage, culture, and tourism since 2014, discussed in Section 1. Under the SCM both cities have been making desperate attempts to carve out their unique identity and city branding initiatives capitalizing on their place-based culture. Finally, both cities offer interesting contrasts as far as the initiatives of smartness are concerned. While Varanasi has witnessed more serious efforts, perhaps because it is the constituency of Prime Minister Narendra Modi and every other brand and private company like to get associated with it. Such has not been the case with Lucknow, which not only lacks serious attempts at cultural revitalization but has also fallen in the rankings on many fronts, like the *Swach Bharat Mission*. Further, none of these cities have made it to the Ease of Living list of cities declared by the Ministry of Housing and Urban Affairs on 14 August 2018. This calls for serious reflection. Sections 2 and 3 discuss the smart city initiatives currently underway in Lucknow and Varanasi. Section 4 critically examines the key challenges and points out the gaps in the initiatives in both cities.

Section 1: policies and practices around heritage, culture, and tourism in Uttar Pradesh

Taking clues from neighboring states like Madhya Pradesh and Gujarat, the state government of UP began to take an active interest in the formulation of aggressive policies and promotional practices around culture, heritage, and tourism. Some of the noteworthy policy initiatives in recent years are tax exemptions to filmmakers to shoot in cities like Lucknow and other locations of UP; huge investments in urban mega-projects, like the Gomti riverfront in Lucknow, as major tourist attractions; promoting religious tourism in cities like Ayodhya and Allahabad; the Buddhist Circuit covering cities like Sarnath and Kushinagar; the Chitrakoot circuit covering cities in and around Ayodhya; and branding through religious festivals like *Kumbh Mela* in Allahabad and also secular ones like Lucknow Mahotsav and Gorakhpur Mahotsav and the recently instituted UP Diwas. In addition, investments are being made in the construction of new places like the *Awadh Shilp Gram* in Lucknow, centers of learning like the National Institute of Fashion Technology (NIFT) in Varanasi, stadiums, museums, and convention centers for city branding. Event management companies, mass media like radio and newspapers, and social media management companies have emerged as significant players in these initiatives with elaborate media plans. The state government of UP has been particularly successful over the last few years in attracting the attention of the entertainment industry, like the Hindi film industry and allied fields. With numerous initiatives like single window clearance, tax exemptions to filmmakers, and taking advantage of its tucked-away-from-the-limelight approach, filmmakers have flocked to the Hindi heartland to have a hassle-free and budget-friendly filmmaking experience. The recent surge of realistic movies like *Tanu Weds Manu, Toilet Ek Prem Katha, Jolly LLB,* and *Mukkebaaz* and many television shows rooted in the Hindi heartland has also helped in shifting the locations of films to the rustic countryside replacing the fancier and often costlier foreign landscapes. Lucknow has further strengthened its position as a coveted film destination, with many announcements made in the recently concluded UP Investors' Summit in February 2018. The most notable of these announcements include the following:

- A film city near Lucknow on the lines of Ramoji Film City of Hyderabad
- A 500-crore film on Ramayana will be shot in UP next year
- Financial assistance will be made available to filmmakers of UP origin if they shoot in UP, and these include Indians and citizens of Mauritius, Trinidad, and Tobago
- Films in any language, including English, will get a subsidy if shot in UP
- More film theaters, both single screen and multiplexes, are to be set up (Lal, 2018)

Another noteworthy policy of the Department of UP Tourism is the Heritage Arc that was institutionalized in 2014, covering the historic cities of Varanasi, Agra, and Lucknow. Unlike the mega-cities of Kolkata, Delhi, and Mumbai that have always monopolized popular representations of heritage in India, cities in UP have remained underexposed despite having a rich cultural and historical legacy. The Heritage Arc aims at breaking this monopoly of mega-cities. A meeting with travel agents and people from the hospitality industries in 2014 seemed to do the trick, and the Heritage Arc was institutionalized. The three cities of Varanasi, Agra, and Lucknow were chosen to represent the arc, as these cities do form an arc geographically. The rationale was to back the geographical arc with a cultural one.

The tourism industry of north India thrived on the golden triangle comprising Jaipur, Delhi, and Agra for decades. A fresh take on tourism was therefore imminent. An official of the Department of UP Tourism stated:

> Uttar Pradesh is an enriched region known for its arts, crafts, cuisine and monuments. The rationale for the choice of Lucknow and Varanasi in the Heritage Arc is that despite being historical cities with Varanasi having tremendous religious significance and Lucknow often referred to as the Paris of the East for its rich cultural heritage, these cities could never really emerge as coveted destinations for cultural and heritage tourism compared to other cities of North India like Agra, Delhi and Jaipur. It is time that the city of Lucknow and Varanasi got their due. The Heritage Arc takes a fresh look at cultural tourism with the inclusion of cities like Varanasi and Lucknow replacing the older vision of the golden triangle of cultural tourism in North India comprising Delhi, Agra and Jaipur.
>
> *(Interview with official, 4 August 2016, Lucknow)*

The department has made good use of social media and event management companies to promote cultural tourism far and wide. The official website of the department was launched on 27 February 2015 and is regularly updated with upcoming events. Among the other practices, the department has aggressively taken to showcasing the cities of the Heritage Arc on a global scale. The department organized a series of events in Lucknow and participated in events globally with the aim to put UP on the global map. The noteworthy events since 2015 are as follows:

- The department held the city's first travel writers' conclave, attended by as many as 105 travel writers from all over the world supported by the Lonely Planet and Times of India.
- It also organized several heritage walks along with the media giant, the Times group.
- The department sponsored one of the biggest film award functions in the Hindi film industry, called the International Indian Film Awards (IIFA), in Dubai in 2015.
- It organized the Taj car rally along the route connecting the Chambal safari and the Bha-Bateshwar belt. This way it promoted culture and nature tourism.
- The UP-Travel Mart is another event targeted at promoting Lucknow, with attendance of around 120 domestic and international tour operators.
- The department showcased Lucknow and UP in the International Tourism Borse, the largest tourism fair in the world, held in Berlin in 2015.
- The department also participated in the World Travel Mart in London, in November 2015.

(Collated from fieldwork data)

The festival calendar of the UP Tourism Department is almost full, with detailed celebrations planned throughout the year. For instance, *Kranti* is organized close to India's Independence Day, celebrated on 15 August, within the premises of the department to showcase local arts and crafts, like live embroidery centers showcasing *chikankari* and *zardozri* work. A sound and light show was organized to ring in the New Year in 2016 and received international media coverage. The department also regularly organizes sand art contests, laser kite shows, and anti-tobacco campaigns. The hot air balloon festival was organized in November 2015 on the lines of that in Turkey and Jaipur. It was part of the promotional trade fair in association with Skywaltz. To promote local tourism, the department organizes trade fairs; notable among them is the *Lucknow Mahotsav*. This particular fair has a two-decades-long history and is jointly organized with the district administration. Similar fairs are organized in other cities of UP, like the Agra fest, Allahabad *Triveni mahotsav*, Noida festival, and more recently, the Gorakhpur festival – essentially celebrating the culture of these places. The *Azamgarhmahotsav* is a small event to showcase folk music of the region. It is popular among the locals, especially the residents of Hariharpur, where this folk music is famous. The department regularly organizes four to five food festivals within its premises: the government-owned Lucknow *Haat*. The mango festival is one of its kind held in Lucknow. This is what the Facebook page of the department said about the mango festival:

> A two-day mango festival will be held on the 25th-26th of June 2016. Delight yourself with the finest mangoes and make this mango season relish able [sic] with your family and friends. Tantalise your taste buds with [a] variety of mangoes and enjoy the benefits of pack away to make these summers #Mangolicious. The Mango Festival will be graced by over 300 types of mangoes and will bestow its glory upon the palette of thousand [sic] keen visitors, especially mango enthusiasts who wait all year long to attend such festivals. Various events related to mangoes are held too, which makes the event lively and appealing to all age groups. #BeatTheHeat and enjoy the delicious summer fruit in its full pomp.
>
> *(www.facebook.com/events/614103465407236/ accessed on*
> *30 August 2016)*

Section 2: overview of Lucknow

Lucknow has its origin in ancient times. The city grew as a settlement around the banks of the river Gomti. Its built form and attendant cultural traditions have been in recorded history since the times of the Delhi Sultanate, through that of the Mughals, reaching its pinnacle during the rule of the Nawabs in the mid-19th century, when it emerged as the cultural capital with its distinct culture revolving around music, dance forms, literature, architecture, language, mannerisms, couture, and cuisine. The Revolt of 1857 was a watershed moment in the history of Lucknow, after which British colonial rulers subjected the city to radical spatial and attendant cultural transformations. The continuity of old cultural mores and addition of new ones rendered a unique character to the city. Lucknow came to be known as the Paris of the East, signifying its cultural importance throughout the late 19th and 20th centuries. The eclectic architecture, admixture of myriad linguistic traditions, historical legacies, and composite culture came to be represented through popular mediums like films and established in scholarly literature (AH Sharar et al., 1994; Hasan, 1983, 1990; Schempp, 2005; Sinha, 2010; Mazumdar and Mazumdar, 2001; Oldenburg, 1984, 1990, 2007; Singh and Jafri, 2011). These rendered Lucknow its place-specific culture and identity, marking its difference from other cities.

Unlike the newly developed capital cities of Chandigarh, Gandhinagar, and Bhuvaneshwar, Lucknow was not a laboratory for urban experiments for a long time after India's independence in 1947. The city suffered because of political neglect and administrative apathy. Without any significant industrial base, the city continued to serve only as the administrative and political capital of the state of UP. The city once famous for its *chikankari* embroidery, cuisine, and *Nawabi* etiquette began to fade away from public memory, except during the occasional election fervor. Culturally the city remained tucked away in the shadows of its past without any significant moments until a perceptible turn in the late 1990s. With liberalization and the onslaught of global forces, Lucknow witnessed a real estate boom and the entry of private players. A series of urban development projects ranging from new public buildings, residential and commercial complexes, and physical infrastructure like roads and flyovers rolled out in the decades since the 1990s. The most notable spatial alterations took place during the regime of Chief Minister Mayawati. Urban design ideas were skillfully deployed to create places like public parks and memorials to resurrect particularized identities and political prowess. It helped pull the city out of its lull and made it a topic of discussion across media, academia, architecture, and environmental circles. Each had its own version of the good and bad effects of these new spaces. The common narrative that developed was that Lucknow made it to the popular imagination of the people and in some ways hit the chords with its citizens by emerging as a modern city, breaking the shackles of its history. The thrust on urban design as a cultural tool continued to be deployed by later governments in due earnest. Several monuments and parks have sprung up during the successive political regimes as markers of identity, reassertion of symbolic power, and city branding like the *Parivartan Chowk* and the *Ambedkar Samajik Parivartan Sthal.*

Since the 1990s, the forces of cultural globalization, aspirations, and visions have transformed and continue to transform the city rapidly. This transformation is particularly visible in the changing cityscape, with an increasing number of gated communities; places of commerce like office complexes, information technology (IT) parks, banks and financial centers; places of recreation like golf courses, private clubs, and amusement parks; places of leisure like spas and salons; hotels; up-market restaurants and bars; shopping malls; and places of entertainment like multiplexes. Lucknow is transforming rapidly amid growing global cultural linkages and aspirations bolstered through the rapid and widespread use of information and communication technologies (ICTs). These are directed to pull it out of its lull and help it emerge as a smart competitive city with global aspirations. It is not surprising that present-day Lucknow is a city of contrasts, with marked distinctions between the old and new. Although attempts to revitalize and conserve heritage sites are carried out by organizations like INTACH, the inner-city spaces like neighborhoods, *mohallas, gullies,* and bazaars carry a different narrative. New scholarly attention to dilapidated inner cities (qualifying them as living heritage) carries a lot of significance for historical cities like Lucknow.

Lucknow has always been and still is the political and administrative hub of north India, second only to New Delhi. Recent events like the Investors Summit in February 2018 and the One District One Product (ODOP) Summit in July 2018 have laid out the future roadmap of the city, in addition to the Smart City Plan (SCP) that has projects worth Rs 232 crore that are currently underway.

Major infrastructure projects were unveiled in Lucknow in August 2018. These include:

- New elevated roads worth Rs 414 crore to decongest the city at points like Haiderganj crossing, Meena Bakery, and Tulsidas crossings
- Flyovers are sanctioned for Sitapur road, Rae Bareli road, and Kanpur road on the high-traffic chokepoints in Lucknow
- Redevelopment of three railway stations: Charbagh, Alamnagar, and Gomti Nagar
- Enhancing airport passenger handling capacity from 23 lakh to 1 crore
- Various sewer and waterworks across the city
- Cleaning of the Gomti River.

(HT Correspondent, 2018)

The SCP of Lucknow envisions it as the new cultural capital of India. To that end, several policies have been put in place seeking to revitalize the heritage of old Lucknow and revive the intangible aspects of culture through recent policies and practices discussed in the following sections.

The Smart City Plan of Lucknow

The SCP of Lucknow aspires to reposition Lucknow as the heritage and cultural capital of India. Lucknow's SCP is based on the following vision: Lucknow Smart City aspires to leverage its culture and heritage by investing in inclusive and transformative solutions that enhance the quality of life for its citizens ("Fast track Lucknow-executive summary smart city proposal," 2016). On the description of contemporary Lucknow, an official interviewed on 10 August 2016, remarked:

> We would like to brand Lucknow as a smart heritage city – a city that has a rich historical and cultural legacy and is also modern in terms of physical and social infrastructure, greater connectivity, advanced information technology with free Wi-Fi zones and a safe environment for tourists.

There are two kinds of smart city solutions that are planned for Lucknow: pan-city solutions and area-based development. Pan-city solutions pertain to various areas of the urban economy, like waste management, transport and traffic, water, and sanitation. The focus is on technological and digital solutions and e-governance.

The smart city blueprint of Lucknow (Lucknow Municipal Authority, 2016) stands on four pillars:

1   Livable – *Jeevant* Lucknow. This refers to the basic infrastructure to meet the demand and supply gap in a proactive approach. A holistic transformation

across infrastructure delivery to provide a better quality of life will be carried out in a phased manner.

2 Mobility – *Sugam* Lucknow. Traffic and transportation have emerged as major themes for citywide interventions. Smart solutions will be implemented in the city in sync with area-based development (ABD). Smart solutions like smart bus shelters and smart parking solutions will seek to provide better movement of traffic, encouraging walkability and cyclability for commuters' ease.

3 Clean – *Swachh* Lucknow. Sanitation, the eradication of open defecation, solid waste management, pollution, and unorganized and inaccessible open spaces have been identified for smart interventions.

4 Prosperous – *Samruddh* Lucknow. Harnessing on its heritage, culture, handicraft, cuisine, and connectivity to generate economic opportunities; conserve the city's unique culture; and showcase it to the world. All four strategic focal points – *Jeevant* Lucknow, *Sugam* Lucknow, *Swachh* Lucknow, and *Samruddh* Lucknow – are envisioned as part of single strategy with components embedded in both pan-city and ABD.

The SCP of Lucknow converges with other schemes of the government of India, like the Atal Mission for Rejuvenation and Urban Transformation (AMRUT), HRIDAY, Swachh Bharat Mission (SBM), IPDS, Shelter for All, Digital India, Make in India, and Skill India. Like in the case of SCPs in other cities of India, this plan also has a similar institutionalized setup comprising parastatals, a project management consultant (PMC) firm, and the municipal authority (Nagar Nigam) of Lucknow. After the initial draft was floated in 2015, it took about a year or so to finalize the project team and engage with various agencies. According to official estimates, it will take another four years to translate the plan into reality.

Area-based development (revitalization of Qaiserbagh heritage precinct)

In Lucknow the ABD component of the SCP offering retrofitting solutions is currently operational in Qaiserbagh in the older part of the city. City-based heritage conservation architect Asheesh Srivastav prepared the Heritage Development Plan for inner-city areas of old Lucknow in 2010–11. This plan covered monuments, *havelies*, gardens, palaces, colonial cemeteries, schools, churches, and clubs that render Lucknow its unique place-based culture. Picking up the threads from there, the present-day SCP focuses on revitalization of the heritage precinct in Qaiserbagh in the inner city of old Lucknow.

According to Srikant Jain, Official, Smart City Project, Nagar Nigam Lucknow:

> The revitalization of the Qaiserbagh heritage precinct comes under the category of Area Based Development. But we do not believe in retrofitting solutions and restoring the old monuments in the precinct only. Rather

than focussing on the spot solutions only, we are aiming at creating greater mobility and linkages of the larger precinct which symbolizes Lucknow's historical and cultural legacy. This place represents 200 years of history, from the times of the Mughals, Nawabs, French and British colonial rule when Awadh reached its pinnacle and evolved as the high seat of culture in the East. The idea is to recreate the Oriental experience complete with cobbled pathways, facade upliftment, landscaping, widening roads, better lighting, garbage disposal, sewage and drainage, greater connectivity through roads and public transport. There are separate plans for cultural centers like the *Ameeradullah* library and *Bhatkhande* which is a music institute and now a Deemed University, one of its kind in the country. We have networked with experts like historians, conservation architects, citizens and taken their views while developing this Plan. The Lucknow Management Association, a prominent citizens' group comprising eminent people from the city has been instrumental in sharing its inputs. We had sixteen public meetings through various stages of the preparation of the draft of the Smart City Plan of Lucknow, created a huge team of more than 60 people, installed apps and websites to ease the interface with people. We have also interacted with institutions like the Indian National Trust for Art and Cultural Heritage (INTACH), Department of UP Tourism, and Archaeological Survey of India (ASI).

(Interview, Srikant Jain, Official, Smart City Project,
Nagar Nigam Lucknow, March 2017)

The PMC involved in the ABD in Qaiserbagh believes in minimum intervention with maximum visibility.

In an interview with the PMC, he explained:

We will restore what we have. Currently there are no drains, no pathways, and the pedestrian character of the *chauraha* is almost lost. Traffic is unruly with no space for pedestrians. We are working to revive the pedestrian character carving out parking areas, pathways and enabling pedestrian movement from the existing available spaces. We are also working towards designing a tabletop crossing, facade restoration of existing buildings, provide electric signage, organize vehicle mobility and work on the aesthetics and beautification of the area. These are planned with simple interventions like doing away with the hanging wires and cables, cleaning, installing dustbins and the like.

(interview, 26 April 2018)

Section 3: overview of Varanasi

Varanasi is a sacred city (known as *tirtha sthal* in Hindi) with ancient origins. The city is mentioned as early as in the 7th-century AD account of the Chinese Buddhist pilgrim, Hsuan-tsang, who visited the city and described it as thickly populated and prosperous. He also called it a seat of learning with 20 important temples, including one of the Shiva *lingas*, about 30 m high covered with a copper plate, and the Mauryan pillar, a fragment of which, called the Lat Bhairava, is presently only 1.5 m tall. Varanasi featured significantly throughout India's history — essentially as a stronghold of Hindu philosophy and belief but also figured prominently in the devotional resurgence during the 14th to early 17th centuries and in later years. Under British rule in 1791, Jonathan Duncan, a British resident in Varanasi, founded Sanskrit College, and in 1853 the present buildings of the college were built in the Gothic style. Among the other local education initiatives, Jay Narayan Ghosal, a rich landlord from Bengal, founded a school in 1814 with British support, and in 1898 Annie Besant, the founder of the Theosophical Society in India, started Central Hindu College, the campus of which proved to be the nucleus of a growing university. In 1916, the viceroy of India, Lord Hardinge, laid the foundation stone of the Banaras Hindu University (BHU).

After independence, the Banaras Improvement Trust was constituted in 1948. In 1951 the first master plan of the city was prepared. The revised plans were drawn up in 1973 and 1982. But according to officials, none of these plans were implemented. Implementation was delayed with recommendations for further revision. The latest plan was submitted on 26 February 1996 which for the first time introduced the concept of heritage planning and proposed the idea of preservation of heritage zones. The state government of UP approved and accepted this plan in July 2001. In this plan five cultural zones have been identified that require special attention.

The Varanasi Development Authority (VDA) under the UP Urban Planning and Development Act 1973 Act 11 and 1973 (State Act) was constituted for city administration and governance at the municipal level. The VDA is responsible for planning the development of the city and is also responsible for the protection of heritage zones, sites and properties, and surrounding physical environment. VDA houses the offices of the commissioner of the Varanasi division as its chairman, the vice chairman, the chief town planner, and the secretary. The VDA has technical assistance from experts in its divisions of Town Planning, Architecture, Engineering, and Surveying. A conservation cell was created within the purview of the VDA comprising four eminent citizens with knowledge about heritage conservation. This cell is responsible for monitoring the preservation of heritage sites. The superintendent engineer, chief town planner, and statistician of the VDA are jointly responsible for the conservation and protection of the heritage sites working closely with the Tourism Department of UP and the central government. The conservation cell works on the advice of experts from an expert panel for formulating bylaws, ensuring their implementation and continuous evaluation of both policy initiatives and bylaws.

Varanasi, or Banaras as it is popularly called, is famous for its unique place-based culture and religious significance to the Hindus, who often call it Kashi. The living cultural traditions of this city are expressed through rituals and festivals, traditional and ancient forms of worship and belief systems, and architecture and built form (temples, palaces, *maths*, mosques, *ashrams*, etc.), in everyday lives of the local residents, traditional education, music, dance, and arts and crafts. The Ganga River, or *Gangā-ji* (as the river Ganges is called in India), is the mainstay of Varanasi. Considered to be the most holy river for Hindus, it is especially sacred in Varanasi, where its course towards the Bay of Bengal suddenly turns north. Symbolically, the flow from south to north refers to the life cycle from death (south, the realm of death, Yama) to life (north, the realm of life, Shiva, and his abode in Kailash). This unique directional change of the river course led to the development of the ancient city, Kashi, on the west banks of the river, facing the rising sun and thereby rendering the *ghats* of Varanasi a sacred status for all Hindu rituals. The city still holds a significant place and is the seat of learning of ancient texts, spiritual practices, philosophical learnings, traditional systems of medicine, yoga, and astrology. Present-day Varanasi is a bustling city with wholesale and retail centers for diverse commercial activities. Currently the city houses five universities, hundreds of active cultural institutes and religious establishments, traditional schools, music, dance, and art forms that have spread to the world, along with local artisan and handicraft products in textiles, wood, and metal work. Globally it is known as the sacred city of India and is recognized as the most ancient continuously living city of the world, discovered and proven through excavations and historic documents. Varanasi thrives on tourism, with thousands of Hindu, Buddhist, and Jain pilgrims and foreign visitors each day. Table 3.1 presents data on population, density, and geographical spread of Varanasi.

The Smart City Plan in Varanasi

The SCP of Varanasi comprises interventions in an area of 1,400 acres in the core of the city implementing the ABD approach of the SCP. The historic core of Varanasi comprises three main zones. On the eastern side, this heritage zone is flanked by a

TABLE 3.1 City profile of Varanasi
Area: 16500 Hectare
Population: 12.74 Lac (2001)
Density: 77.21 Person/Hect.

Urban Agglomeration		
Year	Population	Growth Rate
1981	773,865	
1991	1,000,747	
2001	1,274,000	27.37%
2011	1,621,000	27.24%
2021	2,070,000	26.25%
2031	2,621,000	28.50%

Source: Varanasi Development Authority, 2017.

strip of trees along the sand belt of the river. On the western side, it is delineated by the road that connects the Asi locality to Rajghat via Shivala, Pandey Haveli, Godaulia, Chowk, Maidagin, Macchodari, and Bhaisasur. The 84 riverfront *ghats* cover a length of 6.8 km along the crescent-shaped bank of the Ganga River, from the confluence of Asi drain in the south to the confluence of the Varana River in the north. These *ghats* are characteristic, with unique flights of stone steps emerging from the river and leading towards the city. This whole area can be divided into six subzones/districts: (1) the rural buffer district, the 300-m-wide green strip lying between the eastern bank of the Ganga River and the edge of the settlement area; (b) the landscape conservation district, the sandy-silty loam area subject to annual inundation and seasonally used to cultivate summer vegetables and melons and for summer recreation; (c) the 5.5-km-long crescent-shaped basin of the Ganga River from Nagwa to Raj Ghats; (d) the 5.3-km stretch of 83 *ghats* (stairways to the bank) along the western bank of the Ganga River; (e) the urban preservation subzone and the old city heritage subzone; and (f) the urban buffer sub-zone, a strip of 50 m to 100 m wide from the western road marking the boundary. Sometimes this boundary goes along with the road towards west with a view to covering some very pertinent sites (e.g. Adi Vishvanatha and Razia Bibi Mosque in Bansaphatak). The core heritage area lies within the old city heritage zone. It is demarcated by the path linking Vishalakshi Devi, Dharmakupa, Vishvanatha, Annapurna, Adi Vishvanatha, and Razia Bibi Mosque. The Vishvanatha temple is the nucleus. There are about 70 important shrines and temples in this area. The outer heritage property, across the river, is demarcated by the pilgrimage photo path that covers 88.6 km, starting from the Manikarnika Ghat, going south, southwest, then northwest and covering 108 shrines and temples. Four major temple complexes have been included as heritage units.

The SCP is being implemented by the PMC for the smart city of Varanasi, who has designed it, floated the tender, selected the contractors, and is responsible for the supervision and monitoring of the entire project. The PMC is in charge of completion of the SCP in a period of three years and is accountable to Varanasi Smart City, Ltd., the SPV in Varanasi, with the municipal commissioner of Varanasi municipal corporation/Nagar Nigam at its helm designated as the CEO. The other stakeholders in the implementation of the SCP in Varanasi are the municipal corporation, local bodies in charge of water supply like the *jalnigam* and *jalsansthan*, the Public Works Department (PWD), traffic police, police, district administration, municipal councilor, and the VDA. As far as international support is concerned, Japan has been in the forefront for technological and financial support in many of the ongoing programs under the SCP. The construction of the state conventional center will house trade fairs and exhibitions and further strengthen ties between Japan and India.

The interventions encompass conservation of the historic core and encourage the pedestrian character of the city by designing pathways, parking areas, and mobility in a complete reverse from what exists presently. Figure 3.1 shows the area-based development component of the SCP in Varanasi.

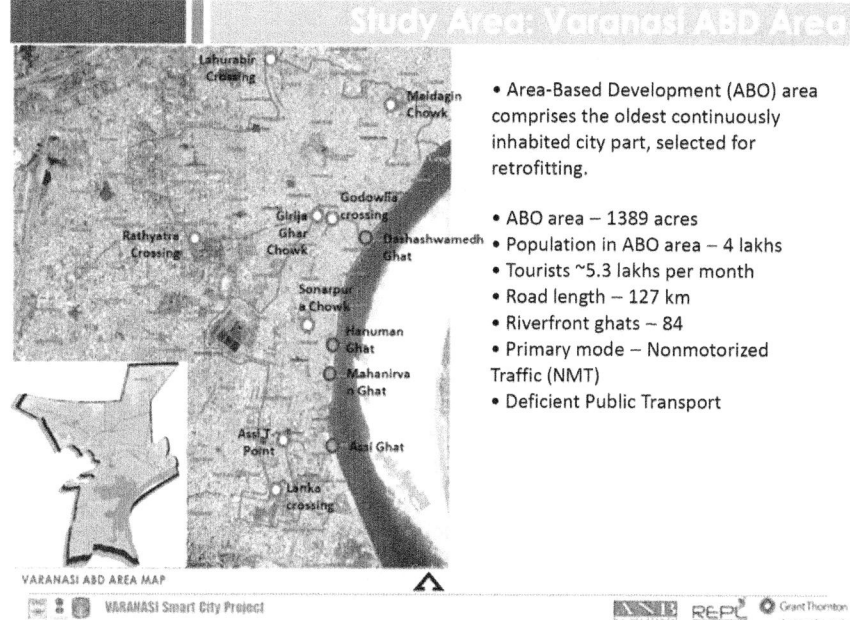

Study Area: Varanasi ABD Area

- Area-Based Development (ABO) area comprises the oldest continuously inhabited city part, selected for retrofitting.

- ABO area – 1389 acres
- Population in ABO area – 4 lakhs
- Tourists ~5.3 lakhs per month
- Road length – 127 km
- Riverfront ghats – 84
- Primary mode – Nonmotorized Traffic (NMT)
- Deficient Public Transport

VARANASI ABD AREA MAP

VARANASI Smart City Project

FIGURE 3.1 Area-based development component of SCP in Varanasi

Source: Smart City Plan in Varanasi.

Transportation and traffic management are crucial components of the SCP. Besides, restoration of the entire façade of the 80 *ghats* being implemented through the PPP model is another major component. Varanasi is famous for its *ghats*, and there are about 83 owned by various trusts. Talking to the PMC, it became evident that without their participation and people's support, not much can be achieved; therefore, the PPP model works best. The ongoing pilot project covers a 5.5-km stretch from *dashashamit* to *brijramaghat* (now turned into a luxury hotel). Figure 3.2 shows the proposed interventions in the SCP of Varanasi.

The PMC in charge of the SCP in Varanasi remarked:

> Ganga is a pious river yet we have human waste and sewage floating in because people are urinating in the *gullies* which ultimately goes into the river thereby polluting it. Sewage is a major challenge in the city. We have to work towards that. For the first time in India we have used 3D photodramatic survey supported by aerial drones that generated geotag photos and data 3-point cloud technology to generate accurate drawings. Kailash Rao Malkar also known as the Dronacharya of India was in charge of the entire exercise. The analysis of buildings for restoration with the use of LIDAR technology documentation was carried out for the very first time in this

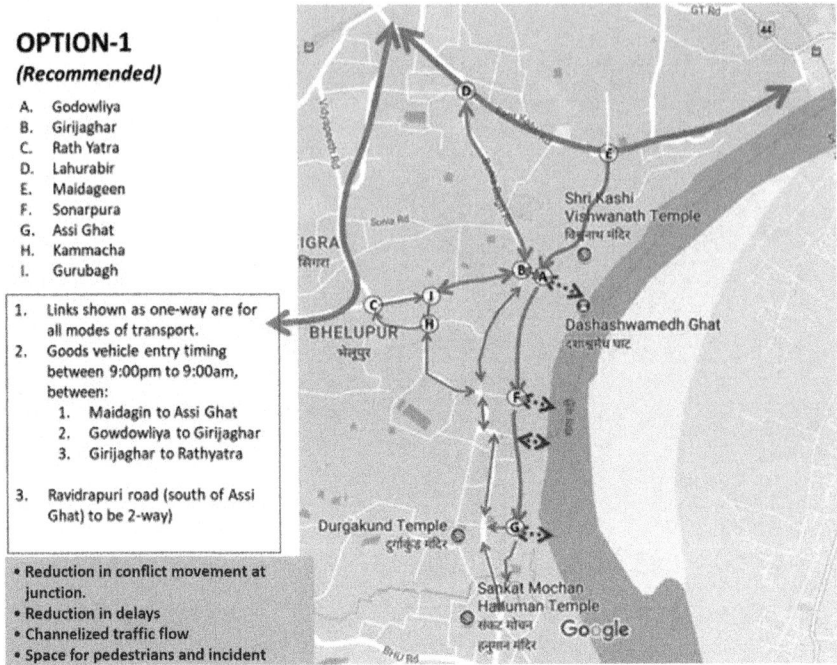

OPTION-1
(Recommended)

A. Godowliya
B. Girijaghar
C. Rath Yatra
D. Lahurabir
E. Maidageen
F. Sonarpura
G. Assi Ghat
H. Kammacha
I. Gurubagh

1. Links shown as one-way are for all modes of transport.
2. Goods vehicle entry timing between 9:00pm to 9:00am, between:
    1. Maidagin to Assi Ghat
    2. Gowdowliya to Girijaghar
    3. Girijaghar to Rathyatra
3. Ravidrapuri road (south of Assi Ghat) to be 2-way)

• Reduction in conflict movement at junction.
• Reduction in delays
• Channelized traffic flow
• Space for pedestrians and incident

FIGURE 3.2 Proposed interventions

Source: Smart City Plan in Varanasi.

scale in India. Very high-resolution cameras were used and the photos were then processed in Cardiff University, United Kingdom. The use of such technology is costly but it saves time and is very accurate. So far master plans developed by town and country planning authority of UP and Varanasi Development Authority never went into minor detailing therefore it clashes with ground realities. For example, streets are 16 to 18 meters wide but Master Plan says it has to be 25 m wide. This is not practical as we cannot demolish the historical structures. So, our approach is to work with the Existing Land Use (ELU) and interventions that can be done on site like corridor improvement and retrofitting. Sometimes the local community is sceptical because of its past experience with government plans and programs. But our approach is different so they have supported us eventually. For instance, in the *Benia Bagh* landscape project (biggest open space spreads almost 1400 acres) we factored in people's aspirations, accommodated their activities especially the refuge market where people come to sell their fare in temporary makeshift markets. The space also hosts football matches and serves as public space. We have managed to incorporate each use and maintain peoples' engagement with the space.

(Interview 18 August 2018)

Major interventions are underway in the *ghats* of Varanasi. The idea is to make the *ghats* visitor friendly, allowing what is termed as physically disabled universal access. The *ghats* will be provided with separate changing rooms and toilets. Until now, the temporary rooms have served as changing rooms with no toilet facilities. During high tides, the water level of the river Ganga rises to 7 to 10 meters and all *ghats* are submerged. To counter this challenge, construction of floating toilets and changing rooms is being experimented with for the first time. The toilets are anchored to the *ghats* and are bio-toilets treated in situ. In the first phase two such floating toilets are being constructed, followed by one in every *ghat* in the second phase of the project.

Unlike Lucknow, where there have been no visible changes since the implementation of the SCP, Varanasi presents a different picture. Since the launch of the SCP in 2015, Varanasi is much cleaner and the streets have been widened, cleaned, and beautified with paintings and art and installation of heritage lampposts. Figures 3.3 to 3.6 show these visible changes collected during the field study between March and August 2018.

Kunds are essential features of Varanasi's landscape, and many of these have been taken up for upgrading under the SCP. Street lighting has improved, as reflected in Figures 3.7 to 3.10.

Luxury liners like the *Alaknanda* promise the perfect Ganga *Aarti* from the Ganges for tourists. The two-floor luxury cruiser is air-conditioned, with lunch

FIGURE 3.3 Assi ghat

Source: Fieldwork.

FIGURE 3.4 Streets widened

Source: Fieldwork.

and dinner facilities for tourists, and was officially launched on 15 August 2018 (Figure 3.11). According to the cruise manager Vivek Malvia,

> *Alaknanda* has two decks. It is equipped with all facilities. The cruise service has been be formally inaugurated on August 15, 2018. Thereafter, we provided cruise service to people regularly. The cruise has live performance of classical music of *Benaras Gharana* like *Thumari, Chaiti, Kajari, Dadra and Jhula* for the tourists on board. In the morning, the tourists on board the cruise can enjoy a view of the rising sun, commonly known as Subah -e-Benaras and catch glimpses of the *ghats*. In the evening tourists can enjoy the famous Ganga *Aarti*.
>
> *(HT Correspondent Enjoy music, 2018)*

Section 4: discussion

This section compares the implementation of the SCP and other urban policies in Varanasi and Lucknow in terms of scale of intervention, branding, community engagement, performance and rankings, and encouragement of enterprise and other economic opportunities.

First, the ABD component of the SCP in Lucknow is much smaller in scale than the interventions in Varanasi. Noted conservation architect Asheesh Sritvastav remarked in his narrative:

FIGURE 3.5   *Chaurahas* widened

Source: Fieldwork.

A mere 60-acre conservation intervention is not enough if Lucknow aspires to emerge as the new cultural capital of India. Conservation efforts in Lucknow could take inspiration and learn from cities in India and abroad. For instance, in Varanasi as much as 1400 acres of core area has been chosen as a site for intervention and for revitalization. Unlike heritage cities like Ahmedabad, there is a total absence of spatial, cultural and visual connection between Old Lucknow and New Lucknow. Salzburg in Austria is another good example. It is a historic city where everything

FIGURE 3.6 Street art

Source: Fieldwork.

is preserved with no room for motorized transport and other things. The organic spaces in the historic core of Lucknow are being increasingly diluted. For instance, the *Phoolon wali gulli*, famous informal market selling flowers is being uprooted from its original location and being shifted elsewhere.

(Interview, 4 November 2017, Lucknow)

Second, the branding of Lucknow as the cultural capital of India has not been able to keep pace with the aggressive branding of Varanasi as a heritage city.

FIGURE 3.7 Lamppost in a street

Source: Fieldwork.

Varanasi is already included in the UNESCO Creative Cities Network. The VDA is vehemently seeking and has already proposed the riverfront and the long uninterrupted stretch of 83 *ghats* that constitute the façade of the architectural zone for inscription in the World Heritage List of UNESCO. According to officials of the VDA:

> [T]hese *ghats* have been witness, through the centuries, to great saints like the Buddha and Mahavira, to poets like Kabir and Tulsidas, to religious

FIGURE 3.8 Improved street lighting

Source: Fieldwork.

FIGURE 3.9 Cantt Station

Source: Fieldwork.

FIGURE 3.10 Entrance gate of Benaras Hindu University

Source: Fieldwork.

philosophers like the Sankracharya and to millions of pilgrims who still carry the light of faith through generations and who make Banaras so special. Everyone who has visited or heard about Varanasi marvels wonders why it hasn't yet been included in the UNESCO List. Visited by thousands of pilgrims, from India and the world over, the old city center today faces intense population and traffic pressures, especially during the numerous festivals held throughout the year. It is today enclosed within the modern city and is being seriously threatened by pressures of modernization and

FIGURE 3.11 Luxury yacht *Alanknanda* in the Ganges

Source: Fieldwork.

development. Proposing Varanasi to the UNESCO Heritage List is our effort in the direction of preserving the cultural and associative landscape of the city along with the river on whose banks it stands. The new shift in the paradigm of UNESCO towards cultural landscapes and in giving more representation to heritage expressed in living and vernacular traditions – as affirmed in the Nara document on Authenticity – gives us renewed hope in national and international support to save the threatened heritage of our city. As Mark Twain said in 1898 Banaras is older than history, older than tradition, older even than legend and looks as twice as old as all of them put together. We feel it is extremely important to communicate that the city administration has reacted very positively to recent moves made by local NGOs, experts and eminent citizens of the city, to propose the nomination of the riverfront *ghats* and old city center of Varanasi to the UNESCO World Heritage List. The administration has immediately activated proposing comprehensive measures for the preservation of the cultural heritage of Varanasi. A series of policy decisions and legislative proposals have been accepted in the past two board meetings of the Varanasi Development Authority and their implementation has already begun. Many illegal constructions, modifications and demolitions to heritage properties have already been stopped. We strongly feel that the enlistment of the proposed zones of Varanasi will give a further impetus to the protective measures initiated in the city. The proposal to inscribe Varanasi further rests on the rare and unique living expression of the religious and cultural importance of the Ganga river whose sacredness has led to the settlement and growth of the ancient city and which still continues to be the main reason for the religious and cultural importance of the city in the country and in the world. The old city has been the meeting place, for centuries, of leading philosophers and religious thinkers of India, who have participated in and promoted philosophical dialectics and debates, accepting defeat and even adopting the new victorious philosophical and logical axioms and reasoning.

(Compiled from meetings and documents shared by the Varanasi Development Authority)

Third, community engagement is stronger in the implementation of the SCP and interventions in Varanasi than in Lucknow. This follows from the fact that the scale of intervention in Varanasi is much larger than in Lucknow. Such interventions cannot be implemented successfully without community participation. Moreover, in Lucknow there has not been any real attempt to engage communities, like the traditional weaver community adept in *chikankari* and *zardozi* work or artisans trained in *nakashi* and *warq* work. These communities are impoverished and are fast migrating to other cities in search of economic opportunities. There is no single vision, plan, or strategy for a place like Chowk in old Lucknow, which stands for everything *Lakhnavi*. Building communities and neighborhoods helps retain the urban fabric that is under threat of dilution and rupture. For one, integrating the local community by first mapping their skill sets, the presence of creative industries (if any), assessing the possibilities of livelihoods, and improving their habitats via connecting roads and basic services like water, sewage, and waste disposal can go a long way to implementing SCPs in old cities that Lucknow can build on. Community and citizen engagement in Lucknow's SCP has still not translated from its vision document. While talking to citizens in Lucknow, the daily struggles and inconveniences resulting from ongoing projects like the construction of metro railway became evident. In her narrative, a working woman remarked:

The dug-up roads for ongoing construction work of metro rail in Lucknow is making daily commute very difficult. Besides, many existing roads are damaged with the movement of heavy machinery and disposal of construction debris. The monsoons aggravate the traffic menace. The routes from Lucknow University up to IT College crossing, Faizabad road from Badshanagar to HAL (Indiranagar), Hazratganj and Burlington Crossing are some of the worst affected areas. Why does Lucknow need a metro rail in the first place? Our indigenous rickshaws and *tum tums* are doing a good job at covering small distances and also in providing livelihood to the poor. But even they are not able to run on dug up roads. How do we commute in a city where public transport services like buses are abysmally low? The construction activities of mega infrastructure projects like the metro are actually killing the *Ganjing* experience of Lucknow city. Lucknow is famous for its fabled, leisurely evening walks across Hazratganj (the main commercial precinct and upscale market with various shops, showrooms, restaurants, hotels and offices) starting from Halwasia up to the coffee house. This intangible cultural dimension of the city is completely lost. Do we have to become a smart city at the cost of our culture?

(Interview, 21 April 2018)

Community engagement in Varanasi is not confined to social media alone. The PMC along with the VSCL are making conscious efforts to engage with communities and trusts to improve the upkeep of their own neighborhoods. These interventions are in the form of awareness programs about cleanliness and reclaiming the lost pedestrian character of the communities through urban design, as well as encouraging walking and bike sharing, *mohalla* policing to curb the growing menace of drugs and prostitution, and provision of better services like water and sewage for communities living in narrow *gullies* who have been without such services for years.

Fourth, the Ministry of Housing and Urban Affairs released the ranking of 111 cities on 15 parameters[1] comprising the Ease of Living Index on 14 August 2018. Whereas Pune, Navi Mumbai, and Greater Mumbai earned the first three ranks, respectively, Varanasi and Lucknow were abysmally low, along with other cities of UP on all counts. The survey has also been done to gauge the implementation of centrally sponsored urban programs like SCM, SBM, and AMRUT. The cities were marked on a scale of 100 (Singh, 2018).

Varanasi emerged on top among the 14 most livable cities of UP but was ranked 3rd at the all-India level, while Lucknow was ranked 73rd. The most glaring revelation was that the railway stations of UP were ranked worst in terms of cleanliness, with Varanasi at 69th and Lucknow Junction at 45th (Top 10 Best & Worst Cities, 2018; Rajeev Mullick, 2018). In other sectors of the *Swachta* (cleanliness) assessments like health, almost 80% of government hospitals in UP failed to qualify under Mission *Kayakalp*, a program launched in 2015 to implement SBM guidelines in health facilities (80% govt hosps fail in *Swachta* assessment, 2018).

Even in the other flagship program of making India open defecation free (ODF) by 2020, Varanasi was ranked very low, at 32nd, while Lucknow was ranked even lower, at 115th, in the city sanitation index because of poor solid waste management. Lucknow generates about 1,500 metric tons of waste, out of which only 30% reaches the landfill, which again is unable to handle and process that much waste. The rest is dumped on roads, lanes, empty plots, *nullahs*, and city outskirts. There is no system of door-to-door collection of waste and disposal. This essential municipal function has failed in the city, especially as witnessed in the monsoons of recent years. To tackle this challenge, SWM in the city calls for a major revamp, roping in private participation on a large scale, including an American firm (Srivastava, 2018).

Fifth, attempts to build creative and cultural industries and enterprises around arts and crafts are underway in both cities, driven by government and citizens. It is worth mentioning that like elsewhere, multinational companies have emerged as the most munificent funding agencies for cultural events. Likewise, corporate sponsorship is a major source of support for many of the cultural events in Lucknow in recent times, thereby confirming that globalization in the form of corporate firms and capital also has an enabling effect in the context of cultural events. For instance, corporate funding has enabled the annual literature festival, travel authors conclave, and numerous theater festivals in Lucknow to gain greater scale, visibility, and popularity in recent years. A popular festival in Lucknow is the Ganjing carnival, which was first organized on 24 May 2015 and became extremely popular among the citizens of Lucknow. The carnival was essentially a musical show by a local musical band and was organized by the Department of UP Tourism. The carnival is held in the main commercial precinct of the city of Lucknow, Hazratganj, which is dotted with colonial architecture more than 350 years old. In association with the Hazratganj Trade Association, the department decided to sponsor cultural events every Sunday that the citizens of Lucknow could participate in. The carnival promised entertainment value along with attractive shopping discounts that could be availed in the shopping districts of Hazratganj. As a result, the carnival met with stupendous success, given that this was a first in the city.

Sometimes the involvement of private companies for city branding exercises can play havoc with the city's architecture. Enthusiastic companies willing to partake in the branding of Varanasi as part of their corporate social responsibility (CSR) activities used enamel paint on many of the heritage buildings. The use of enamel paint does not allow the building to breathe and also has a short shelf-life. Its use is disastrous for the conservation of old buildings, and the present PMC is painstakingly scraping it off, with escalating costs in terms of time and resources that could have been put to better use.

BOX 3.1: LUCKNOW AND VARANASI AND THEIR CULTURAL SYMBOLS

Both Lucknow and Varanasi are the seats of *Hindustani* classical music and dance traditions manifested in a special local style known as the Lucknow *gharana* and the Banaras *gharana*. Many great musicians and performing artists were born here and regularly return to visit and to perform for the public as their tribute to the spirit of the soil. In addition to renowned artists of the last century like Sharda Sahai and Anokhe Lal for *tabla* and Pt. Mahadev Misra for vocal singing, some of the most internationally famous contemporary names in Indian music and dance belong to this city, like Ravi Shankar, the maestro of *Sitar*; Bismillah Khan, maestro of *Shehanai*; Girija Devi and Siddheshwari Devi, acclaimed as vocalists; Kishan Maharaj for *Tabla*; Sitara Devi for *Kathak* dance forms; and many others known for their contributions in the field of music and performing arts. Lucknow is the city where musical forms like classical *ragas* and *raginis* and 12 *khwania* like *Sozkhwani, Marziakhwani, Kitabkhwani, Rouzakhwani,* and *Nawakhwani* have originated.

Lucknow is a seat of arts and crafts like calligraphy, *khattati, Tughrakari,* and *sozkhwani. Chikankari* embroidery, famous the world over as Lucknow *chikan,* is a fine thread work done manually over pieces of fabric. The designs draw inspiration from the motifs in the city's architecture influenced mainly by Mughal and *Nawabi* traditions. Varanasi is a center of cottage industries and textile manufacturing; silk weaving; sari making; metal, wood, and terracotta handicrafts; toy making; and particular painting forms. The silk of Varanasi is famous in India, and people come here from all corners of the country to buy this silk for marriages and for special religious festivals. Saris are still woven on handlooms through indigenous methods and are still in demand. Also famous are the intricate metal works in bronze, especially the statues of gods, wooden work for making toys, and special pink enamel work for wall paintings.

Note

1 These parameters include assured water supply, economy and employment, education, governance, health, housing/inclusiveness, identity and culture, mixed land use/compactness, power supply, public space, reduced pollution, solid waste management, safety and security, transportation/mobility, and wastewater management.

References

80% govt hosps fail in *Swachta* assessment (2018). *The Times of India Lucknow,* 11 August, 2018, p. 1.

Fast track Lucknow-executive summary smart city proposal: Lucknow municipal authority. com (2016). *Official Website.* (Online). Executive Summary Smart City Proposal official website. mc.up.nic.in/pdf/ExecutiveSummary.pdf accessed on 17 September 2016.

Hasan, A. (1983). *Palace Culture of Lucknow.* Lucknow: BR Publishing Corporation.

Hasan, A. (1990). *Vanishing Culture of Lucknow.* Columbia, SC: South Asia Books.

HT Correspondent (2018). Rajnath announces major infra push for Lucknow. *Hindustan Times,* Lucknow, 6 August, p. 3.

HT Correspondent (2018). Enjoy music, Ganga Arti onboard cruise in Kashi. *Hindustan Times Lucknow,* Saturday, 11 August 2018, p. 4.

Lal, R. (2018). Subsidy for UP-origin Girmitya filmmakers. *Times of India*, Lucknow, Friday 23 February.

Lucknow Municipal Authority (2016). Smart city plan. http://lmc.up.nic.in/pdf/SCP_Lucknow.pdf accessed on 17 September 2016.

Mazumdar, S. and S. Mazumdar (2001). Rethinking public and private space: religion and women in Muslim society. *Journal of Architectural and Planning Research*, 18(4), 302–24.

Oldenburg, V. T. (1984). *The Making of Colonial Lucknow, 1856–1887.* Princeton, NJ: Princeton University Press.

Oldenburg, V. T. (1990). Lifestyle as resistance: the case of the courtesans of Lucknow, India. *Feminist Studies*, 16(2), 259–87.

Oldenburg, V. T. (2007). *Shaam-e Awadh: Writings on Lucknow.* New Delhi: Penguin Books.

Rajeev Mullick (2019). Rajeev Mullick PM's Kashi UP's most livable with 33rd rank, Lucknow 73rd. *Hindustan Times*, p. 1.

Schempp, M. B. (2005). Pigs and power: urban space and urban decay. In E. Hust and M. Mann (eds.), *Urbanization and Governance in India.* New Delhi: Manohar Publications, pp. 201–26.

Sharar, A. H., E. S. Harcourt and F. Hussain (1994). *Lucknow: The Last Phase of an Oriental Culture.* New Delhi: Oxford University Press.

Singh, A. K. and S. S. A. Jafri (2011). Lucknow from tradition to modernity. *History and Sociology of South Asia*, 5(2), 143–64.

Singh, P. (2018). Ease of Living: UP Cities figure among laggards. *Times of India Lucknow*, Tuesday 14 August, 2018, p. 4.

Sinha, A. (2010). Colonial and post-colonial memorial parks in Lucknow, India: shifting ideologies and changing aesthetics. *Journal of Landscape Architecture*, 5(2), 60–71.

Srivastava, A. (2018). More private players can be roped in for solid waste management. *Hindustan Times*, Lucknow, 4 July, p. 2.

Top 10 Best & Worst Cities (2018). Top 10 Best & Worst Cities on Ease of Living, *The Times of India Lucknow*, 14 August, 2018, p. 5.

Online source

www.facebook.com/events/614103465407236/ accessed on 30 August 2016.

4

URBANISM, URBAN DESIGN, AND PLANNED HISTORIC CITIES

Introduction

This chapter continues the discussion on how the smart city narrative is rendering the second-tier cities of India as laboratories for experiments with far-reaching impacts. The last chapter discussed Lucknow and Varanasi as cultural and religious cities. This chapter focuses on planned historic cities based on a detailed case study of Jaipur. Historic cities of India like Madurai and Jaipur have always been in transition, often challenging their erstwhile economic production systems and social life. The contemporary nature of historic cities manifests the palimpsest of the past through its urban character and other artefacts. There are several historic cities in India that are still living cities, keeping customs and rituals in tandem with new means and ways of producing architecture and livelihoods. Varanasi (discussed in the last chapter) and Ujjain are two such continuous living old cities. In both these cities, value is embedded in the sacred nature of living. Such cities continue to grow alongside new means of production and manifestation, while keeping the historic values and rituals intact. These cities also have visible layers added to their architecture and urban form during successive political regimes. Likewise, Madurai and Seringapatam are other examples of old cities in south India that emanate from the sacred center to advanced systems of planning of quadrants with respect to occupation and social backgrounds. Jaipur and Fateh-pur-Sikri are other examples where cities are known to have aesthetic and architectural compositional qualities along with civic architecture for governance. The metropolitan cities of Mumbai, Kolkata, Chennai, and New Delhi are examples where colonizers strengthened their trade rights through large-scale interventions. These cities, along with several other cities across India, have transformed on several occasions with added layers, like those of sacred cities, capital cities of medieval times, colonial cities developed through trade, and later as administrative capitals and postcolonial cities. Each layer is directed towards betterment in city administration and governance vis-a-vis the existing old city. The historic cities of India witnessed a massive transformation in the colonial era wherein new infrastructure, amenities, and institutions were overlaid on the existing fabric as an exercise in the consolidation of political power.

Post-1990s urban restructuring has accelerated with economic liberalization and concomitant changes in institutions, governance, culture, and society established in literature (Nijman, 2006, 2007; Singh, 2014; Chaplin, 2007; Shaw, 1999). The urbanization trends of second-tier cities encounter archetypical conflicts and contestations traversing environment, livelihood, depleting livability, housing, and affordability. The role of urban design and planning is increasingly becoming complex and poses new challenges for the discipline. This chapter puts forth myriad examples (with visual representations) of how urban design can be deployed to create smart, inclusive, safe, and resilient cities at various scales: smart areas, precincts, and neighborhoods. Section 1 describes how second- and third-tier cities of India are the emergent urban reality of India with growing levels of consumerism, widespread use of digital technologies and satellite communications, global linkages, and growing aspirations. The Smart City Mission (SCM) launched in second-tier cities of India has ushered in new possibilities for these cities often neglected in the urban narrative of India. However, examination of reality reveals haphazard patterns, fragmented spaces, and random initiatives. These random smart experiments are often not connected to the complex urban realities, especially as witnessed in historic cities. The emerging urban realities of India throw new challenges for the discipline of urban design, discussed in detail in Section 2. This section delineates the role of urban design in understanding and articulating contemporary urban phenomena, and in particular discusses how it could be effectively used and plugged into the smart city narrative. Both urban design and urban planning (discussed in Chapter 5) have to constantly adjust and reinvent themselves to address the new urban challenges. Among the second-tier planned historic cities, Jaipur represents a good example of such transformations: economic and infrastructural restructuring followed by spatial and functional reconfiguration of the city fabric, discussed in detail in Section 3. The section examines the nature of urban form in the planned historic second-tier city of Jaipur in detail. The old economic modes collide with new economic ones, clearly visible in its architecture and street characteristics. The new modes also collide with the laissez-faire economy of the bazaars, informality, home-based occupations, and manufacturing units. This is the reality of many other historic cities across India. Section 4 highlights the SCM of Jaipur and Section 5 concludes the discussion, suggesting the significance of reactive and reflective knowledge towards culturally confident urban growth and a sustainable urban future.

Section 1: spatial and cultural transformation in second-tier historic cities

India does not live in villages anymore. India also does not live in big cities anymore. Nowhere is this urban transition more visible than in the second-tier historic cities of India. These include cities like Jaipur, Indore, Bhopal, Madurai, Mysore, Coimbatore, Ujjain, Agra, and many more. The urban reality in these cities is predominantly dominated by two trends: peri-urbanization in the form of greenfield developments like city extensions, urban development around upcoming highways, special economic zones, industrial corridors, new smart cities, and a simultaneous rupture of the inner historic core. Figure 4.1 represents the urban form of Madurai, a second-tier historic city located in south India.

The urban transition as witnessed in the trends of peri-urbanization and the rupture of inner cities is particularly visible in the physical and cultural geographies of second-tier historic cities that dot India's current urban landscape and are crucibles of cultures old and new, urban and rural, global and local. The cultural transition is particularly visible in the growing consumption patterns of a variety of goods and commodities earlier unheard of. In an interesting article Mofussil. com in the *Economic Times* magazine dated 21–27 January 2018, one finds reference to the numerous e-commerce companies that are catering to the burgeoning demands of these faraway places. The article mentions that Amazon executives say they get 70% of their business from small towns, and the company has set up dozens of new distribution centers. Its archrival Flipkart and other e-commerce companies have worked out the intricacies of sending millions of shipments to customers in smaller towns and cities, chasing down the next 100 million Internet users in small towns. These are big markets for the e-commerce companies in the coming years. This also signals the widespread reach of Digital India and the power of the Internet, satellite television, and new modes of telecommunications. These technologies have spread new awareness, resultant demands, and a

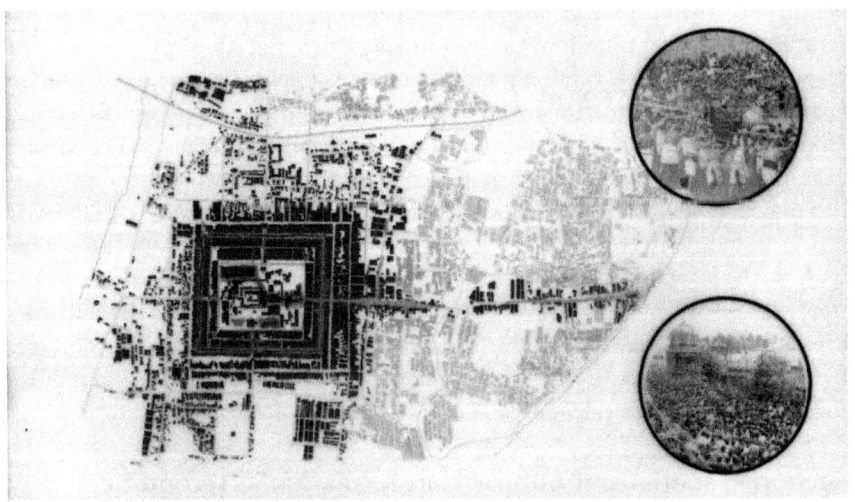

FIGURE 4.1   Urban form of Madurai

Source: Fieldwork.

new class of consumers. These cities also constitute the primary audience of the Hindi television and entertainment industries. The huge success of films like *Toilet Ek Prem Katha, Mukkebaaz,* and *Tanu Weds Manu* – all rooted, scripted, and filmed in the not-so-palatable small and medium town of India – is one indicator of this trend. Apart from their social relevance, these films have significantly helped to bring the small and medium town back to mainstream popular culture. The growing Television Rating Points (TRPs) of television shows narrating stories from these geographies is also an indicator of how consumption patterns and lifestyles of the hinterland are important determinants of content for the entertainment industries tucked away in faraway big cities like Mumbai. A large part of India resides outside the big cities of Mumbai, Delhi, Kolkata, and Chennai. The social groups and communities living in second-tier cities have significantly different entertainment sensibilities and preferences. They have the appetite for consumption and for brands, but they want their entertainment content to be delivered in a language and with an appeal that is relatable. The combination of money spreading outside of metros, the rise of a new generation of consumers with different educational backgrounds, and the emergence of new cultural icons like Mahendra Singh Dhoni, Kapil Sharma, and YoYo Honey Singh more rooted in the vernacular have led to massive changes in the consumption of media.

The SCM aims to transform selected cities across the country into models of technological and infrastructural innovation. Under the wing of the Ministry of Housing and Urban Affairs, every smart city is supposed to feature housing for all, comprehensive public transport, green spaces, walkable streets, dependable water, electricity and Internet connectivity, and citizen-friendly governance. The normative implications of such mass overlaying of digital infrastructure over existing historic cities have far-reaching consequences. The three layers of urban transformative imperatives that work simultaneously on all second-tier cities are:

1   Indian urban planning modalities on satellite cities, industrial cities, knowledge cities, and SEZs
2   Global urbanism imperatives on ecological urbanism, resilient cities, and climate change
3   Smart City mission and consequent urbanism that aims to achieve real-time networked cities and dashboard governance

The emerging challenges of the three layers on the urban design/planning framework may not necessarily have anything in common. There is a conspicuous absence of any structured discourse to find common parameters and interrelationships. The challenges that result from this disjunction in the existing planning paradigm have excluded the primordial and often organic necessities of historic cities of India. The discourse on Indian urbanism can be traced from the multiple layers of history. Each layer has left behind a rich repository of architecture and urban phenomena. Urban phenomena are broadly understood as experience of urban form.

The announcement of 100 new smart cities in India seems justified on basis of the earlier-mentioned global imperatives accompanied with a transparent democratic setup. The new hybrid relationship between this spatial reality and digital technology affects architecture, informality, and everyday urbanism. SCM is not only the subject of mere effective controlling of urban systems but is also the way in which urban spatial formation would react and transform. Urban digital data are regulated through a real-time dashboard in a search for effective governance. The tools and knowledge that are available to articulate the possible spatial transformation of such cities are limited. Such transformative adjustment at the social and cultural dimensions are even scarce at the grassroots level. The issues of urban transformation through normative production of governance are fairly new and face the risk of exclusion.

The classical debate on the dichotomy related to growth of various urban centers in India has been central to many planning debates and discussions. The discussion on development and disparities has been of interest to social scientists for a long time.

The gap between various urban centers in India has widened during the post-liberalization period. The epicenters of the post-liberalized economy are industry, trade, and investment. The agricultural sector, which is a partial economy of second-tier cities, has not only been bypassed by liberalization but also suffered from a decline in public investment, terms of trade turning against agriculture, rationalization, and partial withdrawal of subsidies to the sector (www. tribuneindia.com).

Such policies have therefore further widened existing gaps among urban centers in India that have had cascading impacts on education attainment, occupational choices, consumption levels, and wages. An urban policy that promises to induce changes to reduce the disparity between metros and second-tier cities was imminent. The SCM was launched with that vision. The 100 smart cities declared under the SCM are promoted as imagined urbanism, such as smart industrial, smart finance, smart heritage, and smart eco-city, all of which attempt to appropriate (not as contextual learning) the existing urban realities, with only the cities of GIFT and Dholera imagined to be designed from scratch. The ranking of the first smart 25 cities shows an interesting pattern, as most of them are projected to be part of large urban agglomeration in the next few decades.

Section 2: urban design practice and trends

This section discusses existing urban design practice and emerging trends and patterns of urbanism in the second-tier historic cities of India. Urban design cuts across diverse disciplines like sociology, anthropology, planning, civil engineering, and history to shape the physical setting and built environment. The physical environment constitutes the relationship of building to building, building to people and places, and building to landscape and nature. Urban design weaves multiple, diverse, complementary, or contradictory components into a seamless urban experience – what is known as urban form. Urban design gives spatial direction to the development of the city in terms of its built environment and character. Urban design often faces the challenges to meet contemporary demands placed by the overlaying of new systems, often displacing traditional ones that evolved historically embedded in crucial connections between people, culture, and community.

Urban discourse in India is currently subjected to the imagination of smart urbanism, which again is another overlaying of infrastructure (with concomitant financial, economic, and social restructuring) over existing cities. This new overlaying, in turn, readjusts to various realms and urban forms. The practice of urban design is conditioned by the socio-politico-cultural context of cities. The generic understanding of urban design practice is one that attempts to negotiate the space between planning and architecture, thereby letting the urban designer play the significant roles of mediator and facilitator. As a profession, urban design is quite recent. It is the outcome of classical conflicts between architecture and planning. The role of an urban designer mediates between two disciplines of thoughts, one that addresses the aesthetics of architecture and another that gives direction to city development. The limited role in the production of architecture and planning with respect to the city as phenomena has necessitated the emergence of urban design that seeks to bring virtue to both these aspects. Urban design became an active discipline in recent times, blurring boundaries with multiple disciplines other than architecture and planning. These include landscape architecture, sociology, anthropology, conservation, urban geography, engineering, and environmental studies. Urban design is not an independent discipline; rather it is – or should be – a subset of wider spatial planning. Simultaneously, urban design has also blurred boundaries between community stakeholders and government. The core competency of the urban designer has moved from the core to the peripheries of various other disciplines, thereby expanding his or her contribution to the urban narrative.

The making of good urban places is not merely an aesthetic dimension of the urban form but also about allowing resolution for environmental, social, and economic challenges. The shift in discipline has come about due to various factors. First, interdisciplinary learnings have resulted in the expansion of urban design discourse and shifted the locus and the scale of enquiry. Second, there is greater awareness among concerned citizens and increased knowledge sharing with other professionals on the processes that shape the urban environment. Third, the inroads of digital technologies and social media into our everyday lives constantly bring up urban civic issues (open spaces, safety, transportation, ecology) into the public domain. Urban design has evolved over time and moved beyond its historic role of an in-between discipline and has emerged as an independent discipline by moving away from the shadows of architecture and planning.

The emerging role of technology in city practice is throwing new challenges to the definition and practice of urban design. Every time the city adjusts itself to a new layer or upgradation of existing systems – the nature of public realms, places, housing, and working places – the peripheries also have to readjust themselves. The role of urban design is challenged with newer complexities. The role is further complicated with the overlaying of uniform smart technology over the uneven sociocultural grain of diverse geographies with embedded ideas about resilience, enhanced livability, and quality design-led public realms. Urban design has to work itself and rethink of new ways to meet these new demands.

Section 3: case study: Jaipur

Among the top 25 cities that are overlaid with new and imagined urbanism brought about by the SCM, Jaipur ranks number 14. The top 25 cities were ranked along the parameters of population, gross domestic product (GDP) per capita, food imports, tourism, food expenditure, food habits, food service industry, retailing, and cluster concept (distance from metropolitan cities). The population indicator is clearly numerical and comparable to other cities, while other parameters were assigned values and units for logical comparison.

Due to the controlled and open-ended nature of urban form, the characteristics of varied city networks that emerge historically can be typologically categorized as formal and informal, as witnessed in many historic cities of India. These networks include social structure, economic network, cultural manifestations, and the historical relationship of the city with its own system of ecology. Smart City Plans (SCPs) need to address Jaipur at various scales and factor in the myriad characteristics of its peculiar urban form. The following parameters described next are generic but constitute essential systematic components (with crucial interconnections) characteristic of any historic city in India. These are essential components for making what urban design calls a good urban place. Each of these parameters must be given due consideration in order to make the SCM project more responsive.

- Historic evolution of the city
- Nature of institutions
- Infrastructure and amenities
- Network and mobility
- Ecology
- Livelihood and occupation
- Heritage and tourism

In order to understand the nature of the urban form of planned historical cities, it is crucial to study each layer broadly and then establish the relationships among them.

History of Jaipur

Jaipur is the first planned city of India. It was planned and implemented in 1727 by Raja Jaising II. The city was designed in the foothills of the mountains, and the plan was inspired by *vedic mandalas*. The mythical nine squares formed the base structure of the city plan within which several functions of cities were laid down.

Evolution of the urban form

The city has three gates on the east, west, and north, which are named Suraj Pol, Chand Pol, and Ajmeri Gate. The city is considered a modern imagination of Indian historic cities due to its grid planning structure regulated by *chupads* (junctions) and other important architectural markers. The overall urban structure is formal in nature, as each quadrant meets the next quadrant, with a broad street dividing each quadrant. The nature of the architectural edge corresponding to the broad streets is regulated by height, floors, and setbacks, resulting in an arcade for pedestrian movement. The larger groups of public buildings are located centrally with large open spaces.

The grid structure enforces strict control and regulation on architecture and architectural elements that help maintain the cohesive character of the street edge and *chaupads*. The formal inner streets of each quadrant are in sharp contrast to the main street edges (between quadrants). The inside of each quadrant has a sense of domesticity and varied degrees of informality. Jaipur is in that sense is an important case of Indian urbanism representing both the formal and informal character of the urban form. Figures 4.2 to 4.5 depict various dimensions of the urban form – institutions at the cluster level, ecology of water supply, transportation and mobility, and heritage and tourism.

Section 4: Smart City Mission of Jaipur

Jaipur is the state capital of Rajasthan and is an important center for education, administration, business, and tourism. It is now ranked 10th as the most populous city in India and ranked 31st as the most global outsourcing city in India. The city has also witnessed a rapid transformation over the years, namely, motorized transportation, piped water supply, and the metro rail project currently underway. Jaipur is well connected to rail, road, and air routes and is the most favored destination for tourism and economic opportunities in the state of Rajasthan and northwest India. On 16 January 2018 Jaipur overcame the initial hurdles and made it to the slot of smart cities with allocated funds from the central government, securing a ranking of third place on account of its diversity. The government of Rajasthan initiated the process of formation of a separate company to implement the SCP of Jaipur approved by the central government in New Delhi. The Jaipur Smart City, Ltd. (JSCL), as it is called, envisions the SCM of Jaipur as a city that accommodates changes as desired through the changing requirements

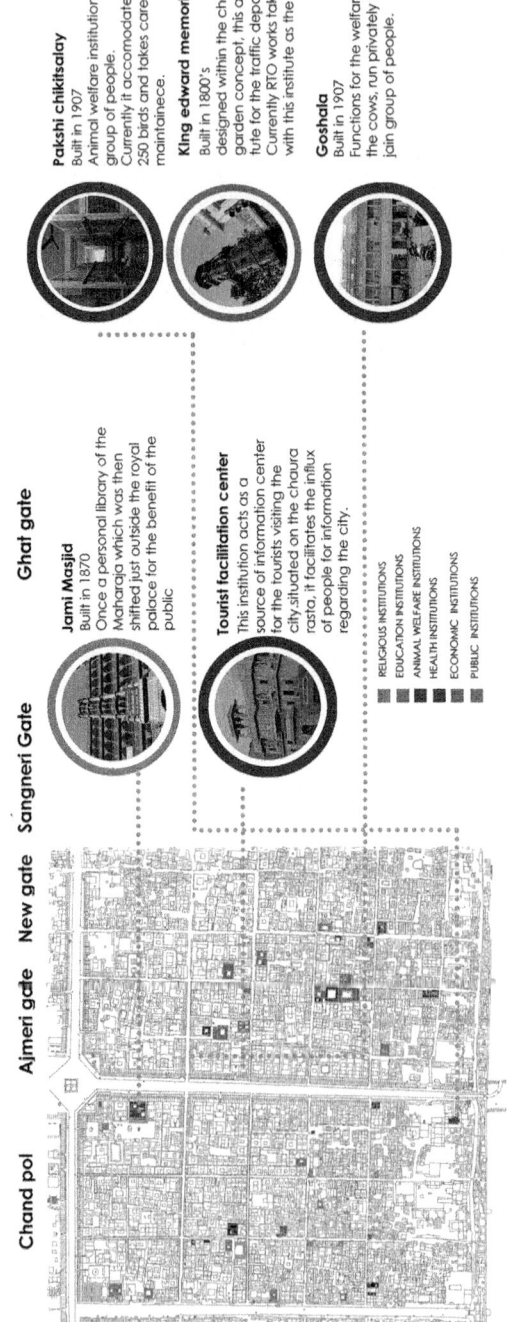

Chand pol **Ajmeri gate** **New gate** **Sangneri Gate** **Ghat gate**

Jami Masjid
Built in 1870
Once a personal library of the Maharaja which was then shifted just outside the royal palace for the benefit of the public

Tourist facilitation center
This institution acts as a source of information center for the tourists visiting the city,situated on the chaura rasta, it facilitates the influx of people for information regarding the city.

Pakshi chikitsalay
Built in 1907
Animal welfare institution run by jain group of people.
Currently it accomodates around 250 birds and takes care of their maintainece.

King edward memorial
Built in 1800's
designed within the charbaugh garden concept, this acts as an institute for the traffic department.
Currently RTO works take place here, with this institute as the back office.

Goshala
Built in 1907
Functions for the welfare of the cows, run privately by a jain group of people.

RELIGIOUS INSTITUTIONS
EDUCATION INSTITUTIONS
ANIMAL WELFARE INSTITUTIONS
HEALTH INSTITUTIONS
ECONOMIC INSTITUTIONS
PUBLIC INSTITUTIONS

FIGURE 4.2 Institutions at the cluster level

Source: Fieldwork.

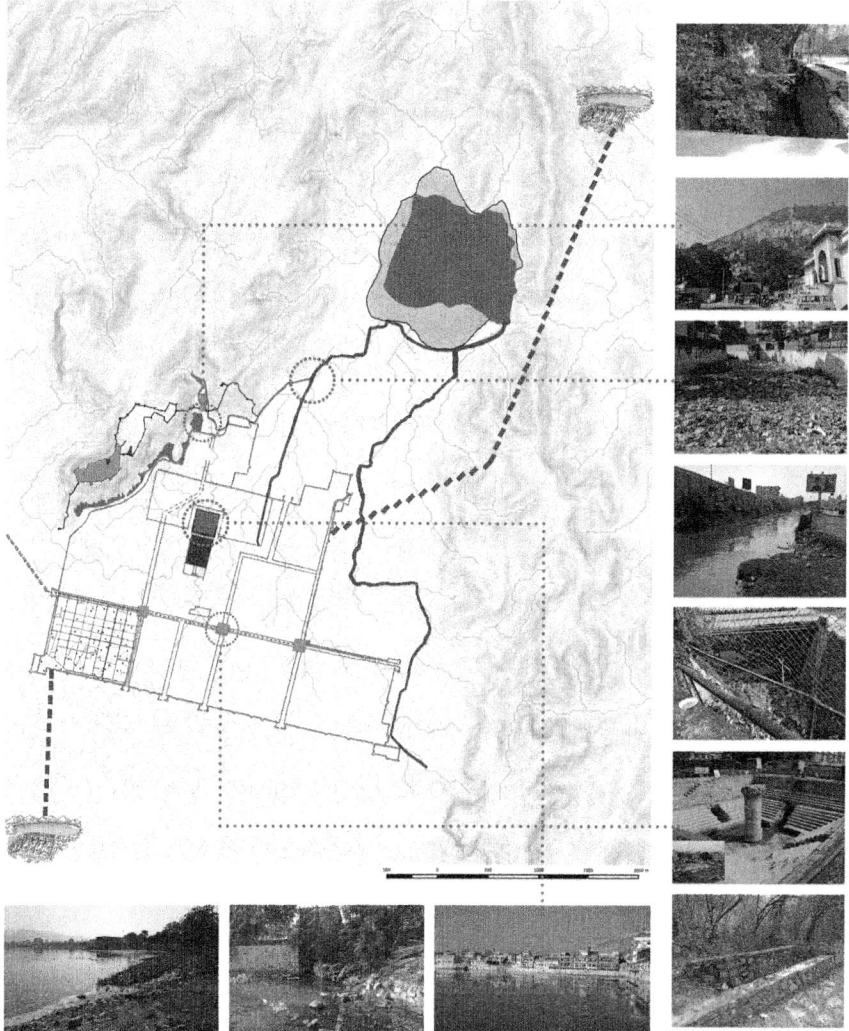

1925 - WATER SUPPLY FROM RAMGARH DAM
1930 - LAYING OF SEWER LINES
1940 - INFORMAL SETTLEMETS STARTED ALONG THE FOOTHILLS OF NAHARGARH HILLS
1940 - CHOCKING AND BACKFILLING OF WATER CHANNELS
1982 - JAIPUR FLOODS (highest water level)
1990 - RAMGARH DAM DRIES UP
2009 - BISALPUR DAM (present source of water to the city)

FIGURE 4.3   Ecology of the water supply

Source: Fieldwork.

of infrastructure, transport, safety, and civic solutions and provides its citizens innovative solutions to make their lives easier. The SCM is currently subjecting the city to another overlaying defined in terms of effective comprehensive infrastructure: effective urban mobility and public transport, e-governance and

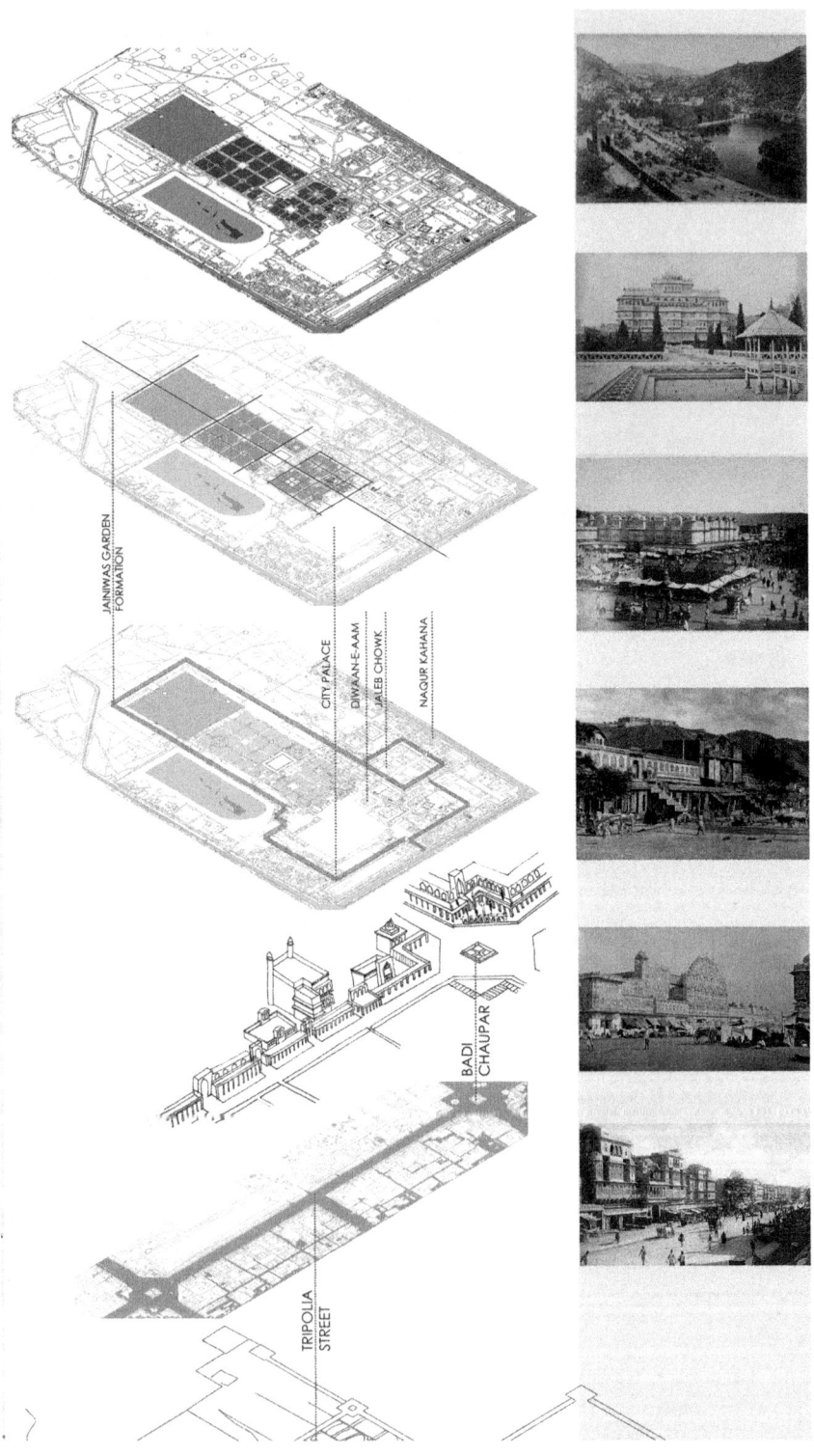

FIGURE 4.4 Transportation and mobility

Source: Fieldwork.

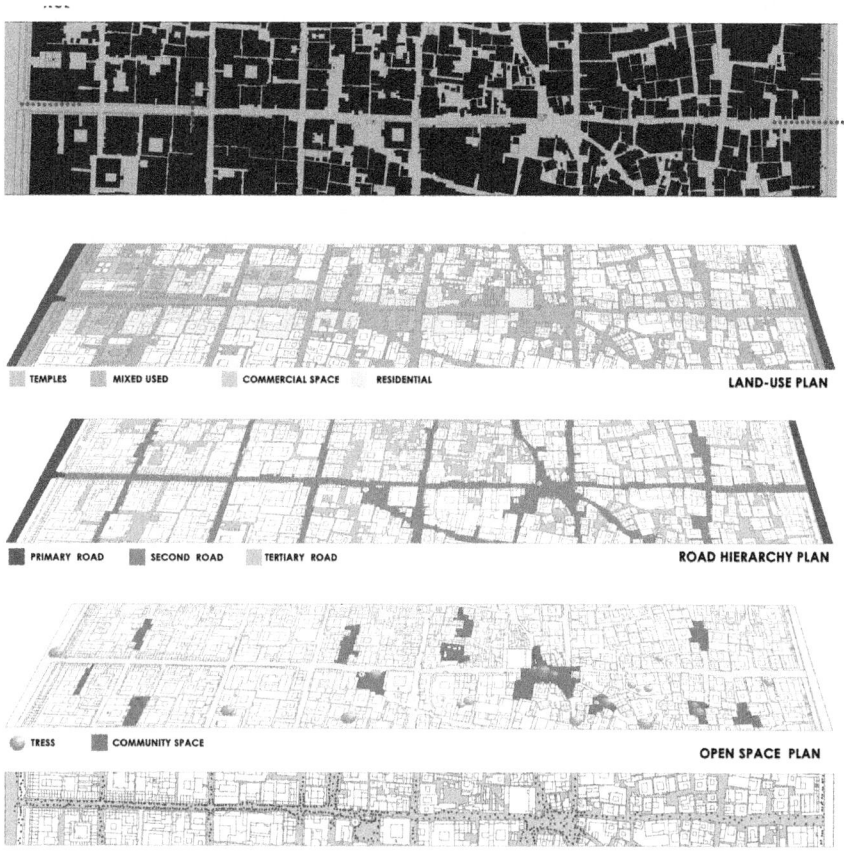

TEMPLES   MIXED USED   COMMERCIAL SPACE   RESIDENTIAL   LAND-USE PLAN

PRIMARY ROAD   SECOND ROAD   TERTIARY ROAD   ROAD HIERARCHY PLAN

TRESS   COMMUNITY SPACE   OPEN SPACE PLAN

ACTIVITY ANALYSIS

FIGURE 4.5 Heritage and tourism

Source: Fieldwork.

citizen participation, economic activities and livelihood opportunities, and sanitation and solid waste management. All of these are categorized in the vision statement of the SCM under four headings:

Smart Heritage and Tourism Precinct
Smart Mobility
Smart and Sustainable Infrastructure
Smart Multi-modal Mobility and Smart Solid Waste Management

The conventional system of the SCM model sees the city as a one mechanical entity or system that often needs overhauling through mechanized processes in order to update it. However, the analytical diagrams of Jaipur in Section 4 reveal that the any approach to re-engineering cities necessitates contextual studies. This contextual study constitutes a delayering process, whereby each delayer diagram reveals the diverse conditions within the city fabric that exist as parts in relation to the whole. The relationship varies as per the nature of the network that one layer is able to create within the fabric. Cities are conceived as consisting of multiple, complex, interdependent systems that influence each other in often unpredictable ways (Inns and Booher, 2000). The uniform system of a dashboard approach may not be an effective instrument in strengthening existing layers that are already tightly networked and have qualitative interdependencies.

As the smart mission is driven by neoliberal economic conditions, it is important to understand that re-engineering of existing cities is not just to reduce to a mere process of corporatizing big data but also to give direction to a possible transformation in due course. The current SCM imagination is driven by corporate interests and ignores the critical approach of urban planners, urban sociologists, urban designers, and urban conservationists. The following model attempts to conceptualize the nature of smartening existing historic cities along various parameters discussed earlier, plugged into a new imagination to enable possible transformations in the future. The model could represent and apply to other historic cities of India with different layers, criteria, and complexities. It incorporates the transformation of local economies, a mobility network, ecological conditions, infrastructure, and amenities, along with community and civic architectural conservation as valuable accounts of history.

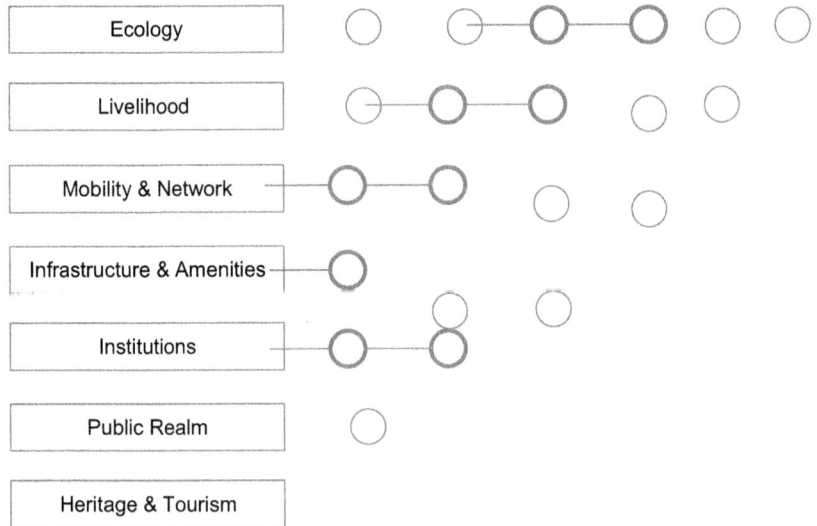

FIGURE 4.6 Interrelationship diagram

Source: Fieldwork.

Note: The Jaipur study drawings were carried out at KRVIA Masters [Semester III, Studio], 2018.

Section 5: discussion: planning a good urban place for second-tier historic cities

The interrelationship diagram attempts to bring about the complex layers of interdependency that are not just absolute but interrelated with several other factors. The SCM model seems to work with the checkbox approach, where compliance is restricted to independent and absolute aspects only. The analysis of urban form reveals that cities defy such absolute characteristics, and they evolve simultaneously following a network approach.

There are several attempts in SCM projects to develop models for inter-dependent, multilayer networks aiding in infrastructure, economic data, and resilience-related research; however, there is little research on how the SCM model can be implemented with a component of the urban form. The component of the urban form comprises both tangible and intangible dimensions that enable a discourse on character zones or the spatial quality of the urban form. In recent years, academic research has made significant efforts towards gaining an insight and understanding of the interdependency relations in such multilayered net-works, and accordingly, a number of models have been proposed. Finding new approaches to overcome complex urban problems has always been of interest to policymakers and academics alike. It is crucial to understand the question of urban form as cohesive units made up of several parts. Each part is identifiable and typologically classifiable and make the cities (urban form) sites for experimenta-tion. In the case of Jaipur, it was found that the cohesive urban form comprises seven components: ecology, livelihood, mobility, infrastructure, institutions, public realm, and heritage. Each component is analyzed as an independent entity to build comprehensive data. While developing transformative strategies, they are articulated as networked conditions. This facilitates the examination and responses of the entity and urban form simultaneously. These interdependen-cies can be considered opportunities to create new forms of urban development, spatial order, and governance that deploy the complexities and diverse layers of networks through which cities are connected. The relation between urban form and urban management (smart city) must be thoroughly understood while devel-oping, guiding, facilitating, reshaping the decision-making process, enabling new sites of experimentation, and stimulating a sustainable and inclusive urban form. The study of Jaipur's urban component has been systematically explored to highlight the specificities of particular attributes of the urban form, as well as their interdependency and networked conditions. SCM and SCPs must under-stand the interests and needs of the community, local stakeholders, their modes of production, livelihoods, and social and cultural manifestations. It is perhaps no exaggeration to state that the smart city process is less about infrastructure and more about harnessing and reconnecting existing components of the urban form to facilitate open-ended, participative methods of a smart way to strengthen such interdependency. Perhaps this also calls for a more democratic and partici-patory experimentation involving locals. Awareness of this social dimension is important in realizing the great potential for socially, culturally, and economically driven smart historic cities of India.

References

Chaplin, S. (2007). Partnerships of hope: new ways of providing sanitation services in urban India. In A. Shaw (ed.), *Indian Cities in Transition*. New Delhi: Orient Longman, pp. 83–103.

Inns, J. E. and D. E. Booher (2000). *Planning with Complexity: An Introduction to Collaborative Rationality for Public Policy*, 2nd edition. London: Routledge, 7 February 2018.

Mofussil.com in the *Economic Times* magazine dated 21–27 January 2018.

Nijman, J. (2006). Mumbai's mysterious middle class. *International Journal of Urban and Regional Research*, 30(4), 758–75.

Nijman, J. (2007). Mumbai since liberalisation: the space-economy of India's gateway city. In A. Shaw (ed.), *Indian Cities in Transition*. New Delhi: Orient Longman, pp. 238–59.

Shaw, A. (1999). Emerging patterns of urban growth in India. *Economic and Political Weekly*, 34(16/17), 969–78. www.jstor.org/stable/4407880 accessed on 10 June 2019.

Singh, B. (2014). Urban governance in contemporary India. *Contemporary India*, 4, 89–111.

Online sources

http://architecturenow.co.nz/articles/shaping-places-a-role-of-urban-design accessed on 10 June 2019.

www.jscljaipur.com/what-is-smart-city.html accessed on 10 June 2019.

www.promarconsulting.com/site/wp-content/uploads/files/STC%20India%20Report%20FINAL.pdf accessed on 10 June 2019.

www.tribuneindia.com/news/comment/development-yet-to-embrace-rural-india/105743.html accessed on 10 June 2019.

5

REIMAGINING THE PLANNING PARADIGM IN INDIA

The trajectory of modern urban planning in India can be traced to British colonial rule and urban planning ideas in Europe and America. This was driven by the search for a rational city, a perfectly disciplined spatial order. The question underlying the need for planning was essentially how the rules for efficient capital expansion and circulation could be internalized in the fabric and form of the city. Early urban planning was essentially concerned with the factors responsible for urban disorder and disease. In India,

> The institutionalization of planning through the establishment of town planning institutions and a knowledge edifice complete with the establishment of civil works departments and engineering colleges and the use of statistics, census and surveys were indeed the legacy of British colonial rule. However, one cannot ignore the fact that the rationale behind colonial planning came from the fears of disease, social disorder and crime that the colonial city posed. The concerns of public health, sanitation, segregation and discipline and the underlying understanding of cities as important centers of economic productivity informed colonial urban planning in India.
>
> *(Singh and Sethi, 2018)*

During the 1970s, globally, this centralized and top-down technocratic notion of planning and planning practices came under attack. Planning was labelled as technocratic, elitist, bureaucratic, hegemonic, and pseudoscientific. The new paradigm called for planning practice to be bottom-up and people centered and one that does not rely on economists, engineers, and statisticians alone. The significance of anthropologists, sociologists, scholars of cultural studies, and grassroots activists who were closer to people was brought within the folds of this new planning discourse. Institutionally, it called for a shift from state to nonstate actors, like community-based organizations (CBOs), private voluntary organizations that were efficient, equitable, flexible, and accountable.

In the 1990s, especially after the Rio Summit in 1992, issues of environment and social inclusion and their impact on the urban form gained prominence. In the later decades, questions of gender, climate change, risk, and resilience of communities gained prominence. Goal 11 of the Sustainable Development Goals (SDGs) calls for inclusive, safe, resilient, and sustainable cities as a globally accepted framework. As the planning process became more and more participatory, new experiments across the globe, especially in Latin American countries, popularized varied innovations in planning practices.

In this chapter we discuss several scenarios and suggest operational frameworks drawing on the principles of participatory planning and good urban places. Section 1 discusses such emerging planning paradigms with the help of diagrammatic illustrations of six scenarios: transit-oriented development, heritage precincts, public space and streetscapes, urban renewal, land use changes, and resettlements of large slums. Section 2 defines the meaning of informality, especially as understood in the urban context of India. Section 3 extends the discussion to slums as the most-talked-about, popular geography of informality. The discussion is tied to the mega-city context of Mumbai, where informality is produced in unique processes, and shows how it becomes an integral part of a large network of the city. Section 4 is a case study of Gazdhar Bandh, a slum settlement in the heart of a commercial precinct in Mumbai, and concludes with an operational framework drawing from the settlement.

Section 1: planning a good urban place: six scenarios

India's current urban planning narrative focuses on land use, zoning, building bylaws, and development restrictions. This includes privatization of developed land, service provisions and construction of roads, and formation of SEZs by land acquisition. In cities, too, the preparation of master plans and detailed project reports by private consultancies has become the new norm. These increasingly promote a new paradigm of globalized smart cities that have no bearing on the traditional social values and people–place connections.

This section illustrates with the help of diagrams six scenarios that require planning for a good urban place in the urban context of India. Most of the examples are from the city of Mumbai located in Maharashtra. These include geographies that have witnessed land use changes brought about by economic restructuring, transit-oriented development, renewal, public spaces and streetscapes, and other contexts like heritage precincts.

Section 2: informality in the urban context of India

Informality – in the form of activities and material presence – is an essential feature of urbanism in India and the Global South in general. Informality in

TABLE 5.1 Planning a good urban place

Large Slum/Resettlement Areas	Examples of areas that need redevelopment a. Shivaji Nagar b. Malwani c. Golibar d. Asalfa village in L Ward
Urban Renewal	Examples of areas that need redevelopment a. Null Bazaar b. Chira Bazaar
Land Use Changes	Examples of areas that need redevelopment from industries to office or residential use a. Parel Mill Land area in G/S Ward b. Industries in Saki Naka K/E Ward c. Mulund-Bhandup in S&T Ward
Transit-Oriented Development	Redevelopment plan around existing/proposed transit station a. Dadar-Parel area in G/S & G/N Ward b. D.N Nagar in K/W Ward c. Ghatkopar in N Ward
Public Spaces and Streetscapes	Examples of areas that need redevelopment in public space a. No specific location
Others	Examples of urban design guidelines in certain sectors a. Heritage precincts b. Buildings

the urban context can be understood from multiple frames as spatial categorization (slum), socioeconomic groups (informalized labor), forms of organization (rule-based/relation-based), and knowledge and practices. The urban experience is brought about with the coming together of formal and informal spaces and activities, as witnessed in street economies across urban India. Other Asian cities, like the overcrowded streets in the Mongkok district of Hong Kong, provide a counter-narrative to the criticism of overcrowded streets and markets: they serve as hangouts for the locals and symbolize the chaos and unplanned spatiality of the Asiatic exoticism that appeals to foreign tourists. Every corner of the inner-city area of Mongkok is filled with traffic, shoppers, passersby, strollers, locals, and visitors from other places. Temporal changes brought about by changes in the street from varied uses – open air bazaar, vehicles, unpredictable mixing of new and old, shops, and roadside eateries – add to the vibrancy and vitality of street life and help in place-making (Lau, 2011). It must be mentioned in this context that the domain of informality also includes the territorial practices of the state apparatus. Noted urban theorist Ananya Roy (2009) argued how the state applying rules of exception and deregulation has informalized planning practices, citing examples of Indian cities like Calcutta, Bangalore, and Gurgaon.

Informal settlements that serve both as work and residential spaces in cities across India are abysmally underserviced in terms of accessibility to water, sanitation, solid waste management, and health services. Despite the economic contribution to the city, urban policies and local authorities remain indifferent to the basic needs of residents in these settlements, thereby increasing their vulnerabilities to impending disasters. For instance, the Municipal Corporation of Greater Mumbai in 2014 pointed out that providing water to illegal slum dwellers would further encourage encroachments on public and private lands (Chakrabarty, 2016). Chakrabarty (2016) also argues the use of the term 'slum' is beneficial, as some networks of neighborhood organizations like the National Slum Dwellers Federation in India prefer to identify themselves as slums, as it assures certain benefits, especially if residents can lobby to get their settlement classified as an official slum.

Informal settlements are often not included in the development plan of cities. Urban planning has increasingly been less concerned about the provision of basic infrastructure and services to vulnerable communities living and working in informal conditions. Land use, zoning, building bylaws, and development restrictions are the major concerns of the current urban planning narrative. It is further observed that privatization of developed land, service provisions, and road building are increasingly becoming a part of the planning process too. While the government acquires land for public purpose, it immediately dispenses it for SEZs, multimodal freight or highway corridor projects with a major real estate component. In cities, too, the preparation of master plans, project Detail Project Reports (DPRs) by private consultancies, has become the new norm. These increasingly promote the new paradigm of globalized smart cities that have no bearing on the traditionally evolved urban pattern and the social values that the urban form contains. This results in indiscriminate allotment of prime public land for commercial use and residential plots for premium apartments in the disguise of affordable housing. This pro-participation of private players in land development, known as the Gurgaon Model in the Indian town planning paradigm, is increasingly finding favor with the local planning authorities. The increasing official and administrative apathy poses as a major challenge to achieving the globally accepted goal of inclusive urbanization as envisaged in the SDGs. Indifference from the state apparatus has also pushed informal residents to various tactical methods to access basic services, upgrade housing, build their own toilets and housing, and in post-disaster work discussed in the literature (Caldeira, 2017; Patel et al., 2015; Appadurai, 2001; Echanove and Srivastava, 2009).

Section 3: history of slums in Mumbai

Slums in Mumbai can be seen from various perspectives. The migrant would see the slum as an entry-level housing to establish his or her household in the city. The urban planner would see slums as an outcome of a faulty planning, policy, and land management system. The economist would see the slum as an irregular organization of informal economic networks that forms the backbone of the city of Mumbai. The policymaker would see the slum as informal urbanization with self-constructed settlements that are commonly represented as problems responsible for the degradation of local ecosystems. The sociologist would see it as social and spatial protocol, born of necessity that enables its inhabitants to sustain their livelihood with scarce natural and material resources. The urban designer would see slums as the marginalization of informal representation in formal urban planning processes and spatial understanding of cities.

Each perspective has its positive side and perhaps huge possibilities in cross-learnings for it to enable urban inclusion in planning, policy, and practice. The larger question is how new methodologies of research and formats of representation of informal settlements support urban design, planning, and political and policymaking processes. How could these processes in turn contribute to the sustenance of informal and formal aspects of the urban form?

Historically, slums have grown in Mumbai in response to growth of populations (mainly due to migration) far beyond the capacity of existing housing. This migration has sparked a steady rise in the illegal occupation of land and the chaotic construction of new slum housing, manipulating reserved land or land within fragile ecosystems or margins such as along railways or estuaries. Many of these homes are made of steel sections, infill bricks, and metal corrugated sheets. None of the slums or dwellers would have a legal foothold in terms of the land or units, or the city's sanction. Electricity lines and water supplies are ingeniously diverted from the main lines.

Slums in turn emerge as an important resource with their symbiotic relationship developed over time for essential services and human capital. The oldest slums house families that provide cheap manual labor for various types of activities: workers for construction sites, auto rickshaw drivers, service providers for repairs and recycling, production houses for domestic consumables, and domestic helpers.

Migrants are normally drawn to the city by the huge disparity between urban and rural income levels. Usually, the residents of these densely populated enclaves live close to their places of work. The residential area itself does not provide employment.

Mumbai knows another reason for the formation of slums. As the city grew, it took over land that was traditionally used for other purposes. The *Koli* fishermen were displaced during the development of the harbor and port. Those driven out of the fishing villages improvised living space that was often shabbier than before. This process continues even now.

On the other hand, some villages were engulfed by the city growing around them. Dharavi, originally a village with a small tanning industry, has become a slum in this manner. Many of the older slums in *Byculla* and *Khar* were initially separate villages, with their own traditional industries.

The growth of slums as informal settlements runs parallel to the increasing informalization of work and economic restructuring in cities like Mumbai. For instance, authors have discussed a process of informalization across all industries that gathered pace in the 1980s and 1990s as industries in search of cost savings contracted out stages of the production process to temporary laborers in a factory or to outside agents and home workers. This was facilitated by the emergence of new forms of casual and contract labor and the growth of labor-intensive, small-scale, informal workshops often in slum and squatter settlements operating beyond the writ of the legal protections and regulations of the formal sector of the urban economy. A speculative boom in property and real estate markets in the 1990s that undermined manufacturing units located in old industrial areas such as the Mill Lands on Bombay Island led to the regeneration of these areas as new commercial and residential enclaves (as evident in the gentrification of the Phoenix Mills in Parel).

Similarly, the formation of Gazdhar Bandh, a large pocket of self-built sustaining slums, resulted from various parameters. Largely it owes its origin to the generic problem of the state body Maharashtra Housing and Area Development Authority (MHADA) for not being able to provide affordable housing at the city level, along with the absence of policy to create housing stock for the urban poor. These, along with large-scale land speculation in the open market and market-driven real estate resulted, in unaffordable housing in Mumbai.

However, there is another specific condition that has necessitated the formation of this large slum pocket in the heart of the western suburbs in Mumbai. The first condition is that of unchecked land that is designated as a no-development zone. Second, the land is situated in an estuary condition characterized by a sensitive ecology. Such conditions are never negotiated within the development plans, either as subject of land or as subject of the ecosystem. Such dubious responses have allowed unchecked encroachment and lately resulted in the formation of the large slum pocket as a spatial illegality.

Unlike Gazdhar Bandh, many of the slums are either designated within the development plan as an open space or as reservation or state body ownership (collectors' land) or private land. It is interesting to note that such slum pockets are increasingly becoming hotbeds for speculative practices around land, development, and expensive real estate.

To address slum housing issues, the municipal authority (Municipal Authority of Greater Mumbai [MCGM]) and state planning body (Maharashtra Metropolitan Regional Development Authority [MMRDA]) have introduced a number of schemes and flagship programs, like the Slum Improvement Board (SIB) and Slum Resettlement Scheme (SRS), and instituted the Slum Rehabilitation Authority (SRA). The formation of SRA (under section 33/10), which is a large body, using policy as a base to eradicate encroachment, has actually further facilitated the delivery of high-end, market-driven houses on the pretext of free housing for slum dwellers, which is a miniscule component of the whole scheme. *Rajiv Awas Yojna* (RAY) was announced in 2009 under the erstwhile United Progressive Alliance (UPA) government and focused on slum dwellers and the urban poor, with the aim to eradicate slums in the next five years. *Pradhan Mantri Awas Yojana* (PMAY) is an initiative of the present National Democratic Alliance

(NDA) II government in New Delhi, which promises affordable housing to the urban poor, with a target of building 20 million affordable houses by 31 March 2022.

The census of 2011 stated that approximately 65 million people live in slums, and this number was expected to grow to 104 million by 2017. The socioeconomic implications of large slum populations on civic services, housing and health care, and social exclusion remain unaddressed in policy discourse or remain exclusive to a few cities. This implies that urban planners will face escalating social, ecological, and legal challenges as informal settlements continue to encroach upon existing reserved lands, fragile ecologies, and disputed geographies. The next section highlights the discourse on slums in Mumbai with a case study to delineate how SCM projects are unable to address, or outrightly exclude, crucial questions of informality that are inherently networked with formal urban systems.

Section 4: the role of SCM in addressing informal settlement: the case of Gazdhar Bandh

This section highlights the informal housing and SCM capabilities in mapping, documenting, analyzing, and making an informed decision process by self-organized slum communities for the provision of adequate housing, given its incremental nature. These are examined in the empirical context of Gazdhar Bandh as case study.

Gazdhar Bandh, a densely populated slum community located in the western suburbs of Mumbai, is one such case. Walking through the narrow lanes and streets of this thickly populated slum community in Mumbai's bustling commercial district, one may not become aware of its informal conditions. The dense social life, ongoing economic activities, and thickly populated residential and working spaces are actually the outcome of unique connections between people and places for three or more decades. This thriving everyday urbanism renders place-based visual identity to this urban space yet remains informal and excluded from the master plan.

Total Rooms: 12,000
Total Illegal Rooms: 1800
Total Registered with MHADA: 10200
(This means that a Slum Photo Pass Certificate in Maharashtra has been provided by the SRA.)
Total Population Appx: 65,000 (90% Hindu from Uttar Pradesh and Maharashtra)
Occupation: Auto Drivers
Service (Watchmen, Drivers, Office Attendants, Courier Boys, Delivery Boys)
Local Shop: Building Contractors and Laborers

Tiffin Service, *Papad* and Bread Making

Mechanics (Automobiles, Air Conditioner, Television, and Computer Repair Work)

Located in estuary conditions, the residents of Gazdhar Bandh are exposed to impending environmental disasters and health hazards until they are immediately addressed. Figure 5.1 shows the untreated waste and debris in Gazdhar Bandh and Figure 5.2 shows the slum site covered during the study.

FIGURE 5.1 Untreated waste and debris

Source: Fieldwork.

FIGURE 5.2 Gazdhar Bandh slum site covered during the field study

Source: Fieldwork.

Unplanned growth and haphazard aesthetics can be greatly altered with the help of locals and a few corrective measures, imaginative designs, and planning innovation.

In 2006, floods in Mumbai exposed the city's vulnerability, crumbling infrastructure, lack of coordination among government departments, and lack of preparedness to deal with disasters. Existing literature establishes that coastal mega-cities like Mumbai will be exposed to risks associated with climate changes like rising sea level, heat waves, tropical cyclones, and storm surges, besides changes in rainfall (Hallegate et al., 2010; Stacey and Barber, 2007). Therefore, climate is becoming an increasingly important challenge as it starts to eat into India's high economic growth rates and seriously affects the lives and livelihoods of millions of people (Revi, 2008: 207). Since 2005, the MCGM established a Disaster Management Department, prepared a special plan for the monsoons, and planned for better departmental coordination during rescue operations. The existing program in Mumbai focuses on post-disaster operations and largely ignores disaster risk mitigation strategies to reduce vulnerabilities that are inextricably connected with the everyday lives of residents living and working in informal settlements dotting the city. The most crucial of these include poor solid waste management practices, unsanitary garbage disposals into streams and estuaries that have been reduced to *nullas* (adapted from the Hindi word meaning watercourse) – especially as witnessed in the slum site chosen for this study – and open drains, resulting in clogging and eventual flooding. What is also missing in the existing disaster management program is the lack of integration of city residents, especially slum communities, into the design, planning, and governance processes of the city as stakeholders. The idea of a local area plan (LAP – participatory approach) was first proposed in the Development Plan of Mumbai 2014–34. Implemented at the administrative ward level of the city (microcosm of urban governance), LAP allows planning for urban renewal, housing, mixed-use development, and civic amenities at the locality level with the help of local residents and stakeholders. The Union Housing and Urban Affairs Ministry has recently relaunched the LAP and Town Plan Schemes (TPS) for 25 smart cities in India in 2018 to accelerate the resolution of area-based infrastructure issues. This announcement also includes central assistance of Rs 50 crore for implementation of LAP and TPS. According to reports, the assistance will be released in three installations: 20% with the submission of a preliminary proposal and 40% during the submission of a final plan. LAP and TPS are formulated under the Atal Mission for Rejuvenation and Urban Transformation (AMRUT), 2015, to enable planning for developing infrastructure in brownfield areas and greenfield areas, respectively (eletsonline.com, 2018).

Still in its initial stages, the LAP provides opportunities for localized planning experimentations that could eventually inform the city planning process. The LAP is envisaged as an intermediate level of planning which would address place-specific issues of the city. Place-specific concerns include redevelopment plans for large slum or resettlement areas and for urban renewal, as well as plans for areas undergoing land use changes and transit-oriented development. LAP also calls for area-specific planning strategies for heritage precincts, designs, and development of distinctive public spaces and streetscapes. It perhaps makes sense in the mega-city context of Mumbai, whose diverse geography, history, and communities necessitate an alternative approach for their inclusion in the planning process, which is currently silent on risks to environmental disasters and consequently invites citizens to formulate their own strategies. The provision of the LAP is a bottom-up approach operationalized at the administrative ward level wherein making, transforming, and directing development are possible in consultation with multiple stakeholders and the residents themselves. The LAP, by definition, is based on local needs and subsidizes the notion of a master plan and drawing-board approach. It is therefore a good starting point to incorporate area-specific design strategies developed in consultation with the community, factoring in their risks and ways of mitigation. Based on our case study in Gazdhar Bandh slum, we suggest an operational framework in Figure 5.3 that could be plugged into the LAP, drawing on the principles of participatory planning and good urban place, engaging multiple stakeholders. The rationale of this framework is that conventionally master plans drawn in the city have not taken cognizance of informal settlements. This is despite the fact that informality is a quintessential feature of the urban condition in most Indian cities.

Once the operational framework is established, it shall enable the process to articulate various conditions that exist within the slum communities. Those conditions vary from residents' associations, illegal landlords, manufacturing unit owners, shop owners, sociocultural backgrounds, user groups, and demographic data, along with the system that operates the entire network within the slum settlements, namely, physical infrastructure, solid waste disposal systems, existing livelihoods, etc. The next level of analysis shall be carried out in understanding the land topography and profile, watershed and vegetations (mangroves), and other ecological features of the site. The overall interdependency of data shall allow the LAP to create awareness and articulate the nature of the problems and their relationship with the issues at large. The LAP shall enable the process as shown in Figure 5.4, which explains the process of engagement in executing the action plan with focused discussion on issues.

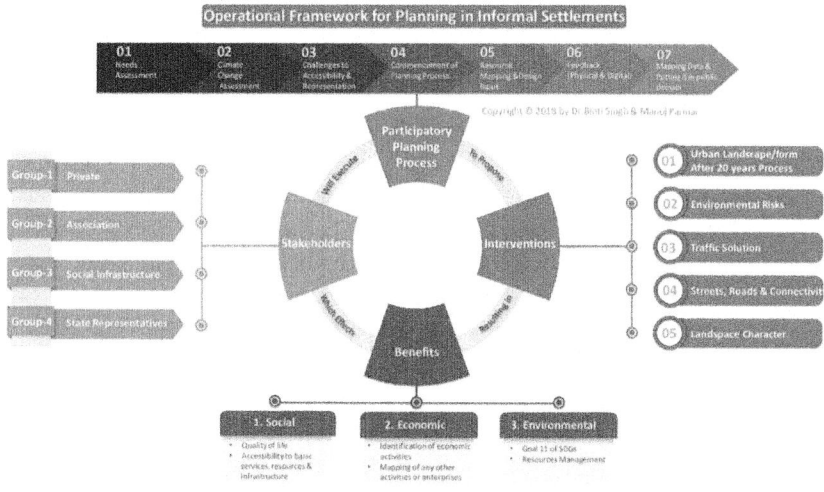

FIGURE 5.3 Operational framework for planning informal settlements

Source: Fieldwork.

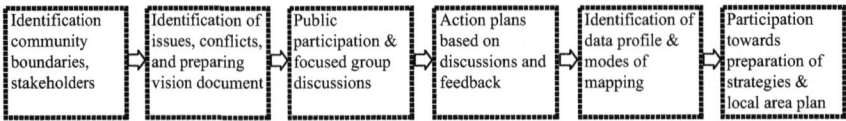

FIGURE 5.4 Local area planning process

Source: Fieldwork.

Once the process of an action plan is in place, it shall help in gathering the nature of the data (data profile) and various modes of mapping. The segregation and integration of data shall, in turn, help create various participatory groups, both small and large. The final stage of the LAP will focus on the priority action plan that enables the process towards the execution of the proposal in stages to make the participatory approach not only effective but also representative of environmental, social, and economic equities.

BOX 5.1: A NOTE ON GOOD URBAN PLACES

How do we design our cities for urbanity or good urban places is the question that urban designers and sociologists have been debating for decades. Scholars of urban design and planning have time and again defined and redefined the meaning of place as that having a structure and an underlying dynamic of activity. Lynch (1960) wrote of qualities like vitality, sense, fit, access, and control, which urban design should seek to achieve and create a sense of place. Alexander (1979) spoke of the quality without a name, defined in terms of the recurring and interlocking patterns of events and meanings in buildings, spaces, and places. A vital city is one that successfully fulfils the needs of its inhabitants within a safe environment and allows maximum scope for activity. A sensible city is organized so that its residents can perceive and understand the city's form and functions: its legibility. An accessible city allows people of all ages and backgrounds to gain the activities, resources, services, and information that they need. And a city with good control is arranged so that citizens have a say in the management of the spaces in which they work and reside. Barry Sherman (1988 in Montgomery, 1998) provided a checklist of urban success indicators that includes a list of qualities or characteristics of successful urban places:

1 Planning will be invisible and the results will look natural, as though they happened of their own accord.
2 There will be interesting and stimulating shapes.
3 The familiarity of streets and street life will be celebrated.

4   There will be secret places which, once discovered, grow on you, making you look deeper to find more.

5   There will be surprises to keep citizens awake, provide topics of conversation, and prevent ennui.

6   Experiment will be encouraged, and there will be exciting things to do.

7   There will be areas and opportunities for informal, casual meetings to take place, including warm and friendly bars and pubs.

8   Food and drink will be a treat, and people will be able to purchase and consume it at varying prices and degrees of leisure.

9   There will be a variety of comfortable places to sit and wait – a city worth living in has to be a city worth sitting in.

10 There will be a good balance between the need to prevent loneliness and the need to preserve anonymity and privacy.

11 Changing seasons will not draw attention away from the sterner pursuits of daily life, but rather will be an integral part of a continually changing city, and celebrated as such.

12 The senses will be heightened: affection/friendliness/hospitality, a sense of belonging, historical and cultural continuity, a sense of fun/humor, opportunities for gossip, open-mindedness, vitality, fantasy, flamboyance, color, and beauty/aesthetic stimulus.

Source: Sherman (1988) in Montgomery (1998).

It is evident from the list in Box 5.1 that good urban places necessarily mean to create better connections with people and their cultural practices and enable the saturation of social life. In other words, good urban places reverse the deurbanizing processes and provide fruitful engagements and meanings to urbanism. This is not an exhaustive list and can be added upon, modified, and adjusted to contextual specificities. Indian cities would have to develop their own set of qualitative benchmarks and indicators to define desired, sustainable, and inclusive urbanity.

BOX 5.2: PARTICIPATORY URBAN PLANNING

While creating a good urban place, complete with diversity, cultural heritage, and sensitivity to the users being the larger goal, revisiting the processes of conventional urban planning is one of the means to attain this objective. The right to city has been put into practice in urban India through activisms, movements, and campaigns and has helped inform urban policy and city planning in significant ways. The scraping of the draft Development Plan of Mumbai 2014–34 and other forms of citizen-driven campaigns and movements for services, safety, and accessibility in contemporary Indian cities confirms what Manuel Castells wrote in his seminal book, *The City and the Grassroots* (1983), that grassroots mobilization has been a crucial factor in the shaping of the city, as well as the decisive element in urban innovation against prevailing social interests (Castells, 1983: 318). Movements themselves may not be direct agents of structural social change, but symptoms of resistance to the social domination, having major effects on cities and societies and transforming urban meanings whereby use values, autonomous local cultures, and decentralized participatory democracy are respected (Castells, 1983: 319–20). Progressive-minded planning theorists like John Friedmann (2010) and Shatkin (2002) have been ardent advocates of the critical role played by grassroots movements. They argue that the key principle of planning is that no group can be completely free until freedom from the oppression has been achieved for every group. Thus, the primary goal of planning is to reshape the existing structure to emancipate oppressed groups from established power, which resides more often than not in the state. Radical planning scholarship is therefore critical of the modernist planning paradigm operating through a centralized government that privileges dominant power structures and systematically excludes marginalized people. It encourages a new understanding that views grassroots activities and their informal practices as the major agent of urban and community planning. Some scholars advocating for radical thinking illustrate how the everyday practices of grassroots groups and marginalized communities foment de facto community and urban development (Beard, 2003; Miraftab and Wills, 2005), how grassroots groups contribute to building strong democracies (Appadurai, 2001) and that citizenship is not endowed by the state but rather grows through the insurgent practices of oppressed, marginalized groups (Holston, 1998), and how insurgent or radical planning represents struggles between the state and the people to define the meaning of the city and of citizenship (Shatkin, 2002: 301). Alternative, radical, participatory, and equity-based planning perspectives could work best on the contested urban terrain of India, as there is a focus on multiple historical trajectories, political ideologies, and cultural diversities with the voice of different socioeconomic groups at the very core.

Section 5: conclusion

Informality, represented as street economies and slums, is integral to the urban condition of India. It is the cumulative outcome of policy and practice of neoliberal governance wherein the state withdraws to the background, leaving the decisions of urban development in the hands of business interests and private players. The slum, a quintessential feature of India's urban reality, represents informal work and habitat conditions. It refers to settlements characterized by at least some of the following features: a lack of formal recognition on the part of local government of the settlement and its residents, the absence of secure tenure for residents, inadequacies in provision for infrastructure and services, overcrowded and substandard dwellings, and location on land less than suitable for occupation (Chakrabarty, 2016: 554). Slums in cities across India are abysmally underserviced in terms of accessibility to water, sanitation, solid waste management, and health services. Slums have formed an integral part of the city of Mumbai as living and working units and providing services to the rest of the city. Slums contribute to the city's economy by housing several and varied small-scale industries and micro-enterprises. They also attract migrant workers with the promise of employment and economic opportunities. Slums adjust and adapt to the formal system of housing and economic policy of the state and the city, like the SRA in Mumbai.

Contrary to this apocalyptic and dystopian image, the slum, ubiquitous of the mega-city of the Global South, is also presented in a positive light as a space for political agency and economic entrepreneurialism. In his description, Benjamin (2000) describes Viswas Nagar, a slum in east Delhi, as India's largest cluster, manufacturing domestic-grade cables and conductors. The 2,000, mostly home-based, enterprises created 25,000 direct jobs in 1991 and supported a further 35,000 indirect ones, which comes from the main production system and also from other spinoffs, including firms putting together the capital machinery required for the purpose; cycle rickshaws transporting small batches from one factory to another, selling small batches of chemicals and raw stock; an extensive plastics recycling industry; and an intensive real estate and construction industry where plot owners build rooms to rent out to entrepreneurs to enable them to start production and also for worker housing.

This positive reading of the slum as a territory of habitation, enterprise, and politics opens up new theorizations of Southern cities that do not fit the global cities paradigm as command and control centers, yet are significant in their own right. So, the slum becomes a theory (Rao, 2006) with new theoretical paradigms like subaltern urbanism (Roy, 2011) that recognizes them as places of poverty, political agency, and enterprise.

Slums also represent good examples of self-organized housing. Instead of providing for new housing units as envisaged in various schemes, we argue for the provision of basic services like water, sanitation, and solid waste management. These could go a long way to plugging them into the formal geographies of the city. Elsewhere, we argued that the most prominent type of housing redevelopment that dictates the real estate market in Mumbai today is the redevelopment of slum pockets. Typically, slum pockets emerged on reserved land, open spaces, and margins within the suburbs. The state government of Maharashtra replaced the Maharashtra Slum Areas (Improvement, Clearance and Redevelopment) Act, 1971 with the SRA in 1995, with a special committee constituting planning, architecture, and social services. The redevelopment of slum pockets has been most pronounced in Nehru Nagar, Khotwadi, Khar Danda, Behram Baug, Ghazdhar Bandh, and Golibar areas of Mumbai. Incidentally, most of these pockets are located near prominent areas and are well networked within the suburbs. The Urban Development Notification under the Maharashtra Regional Town Planning Act (MRTP) Act 1966, section 154, has stated that slums with a density of more than 650 tenements per hectare are allowed to have a floor space index (FSI) of 4 as stipulated in the SRA Act, 1995, whereas those with lower densities shall have an FSI of 3. The high-density slum pockets are more prominent in the redevelopment narrative because of higher sale incentives and profits (Singh and Parmar, 2017).

We also noted that slum neighborhoods are produced every day incrementally and are generally inclusive, although messy, dysfunctional, and substandard. They are also the realm for work, recreation, and education. Such multipurposeness is missing from the new neighborhoods, with their exclusive focus on modern, expensive, and potentially alienating design. The questions of infrastructure and hygiene conditions of redeveloped slums also remain unaddressed. The urban design and architectural imagination discounts any other imagination of the house or housing processes that are prevalent in our cities. New imaginations about cities cannot ignore this quintessential reality. Current urban renewal processes must explore, in a much deeper and extended way, the typological possibilities of housing for the urban poor in our cities.

References

Alexander, C. (1979). *The Timeless Way of Building* (Vol. 1). New York: Oxford University Press.

Appadurai, A. (2001). Deep democracy: urban governmentality and the horizon of politics. *Environment and Urbanization*, 13(2), 23–43.

Beard, V. A. (2003). Learning radical planning: the power of collective action. *Planning Theory*, 2(1), 13–35.

Caldeira, T. P. (2017). Peripheral urbanization: autoconstruction, transversal logics, and politics in cities of the global South. *Environment and Planning D: Society and Space*, 35(1), 3–20.

Castells, M. (1983). *The City and the Grassroots. A Cross-Cultural Theory of Urban Social Movements* (No. 7). Berkeley: University of California Press.

Chakrabarty, A. (2016). Of slime moulds and smart slums – Kolkata informal settlements and the tale of a failed canal reclamation project. *Environment and Urbanization*, 28(2), 553–68.

Echanove, M. and R. Srivastava (2009). Taking the slum out of "Slumdog". *The New York Times*, 21 February, A21.

Friedmann, J. (2010). Place and place-making in cities: a global perspective. *Planning Theory & Practice*, 11(2), 149–65. doi:10.1080/14649351003759573

Hallegatte, S. et al. (2010). *Flood Risks, Climate Change Impacts and Adaptation Benefits in Mumbai: An Initial Assessment of Socio-Economic Consequences of Present and Climate Change Induced Flood Risks and of Possible Adaptation Options* (OECD Environment Working Papers No. 27). OECD Publishing.

Holston, J. (1998). Spaces of insurgent citizenship. *Making the Invisible Visible: A Multicultural Planning History*, 2, 37–56.

Lau, S. S. Y. (2011). The dogma of Hong Kong urbanism. *Journal of Asian Urbanism*, (4), 20–21, March.

Lynch, K. (1960). *The Image of the City*. Cambridge, MA: The MIT Press.

Miraftab, F. and S. Wills (2005). Insurgency and spaces of active citizenship: the story of Western Cape anti-eviction campaign in South Africa. *Journal of Planning Education and Research*, 25(2), 200–17.

Montgomery, J. (1998). Making a city: urbanity, vitality and urban design. *Journal of Urban Design*, 3(1), 93–116.

Patel, S. et al. (2015). We beat the path by walking: how the women of Mahila Milan in India learned to plan, design, finance and build housing. *Environment & Urbanization*, 28(1), 223–40. doi:10.1177/0956247815617440.

Revi, A. (2008). Climate change risk: an adaptation and mitigation agenda for Indian cities. *Environment and Urbanization*, 20(1), 207–229.

Rao, V. (2006). Slum as theory: the South/Asian city and globalization. *International Journal of Urban and Regional Research*, 30(1), 225–32.

Roy, A. (2009). Why India cannot plan its cities: informality, insurgence and the idiom of urbanization. *Planning Theory*, 8(1), 76–87.

Roy, A. (2011). Slumdog cities: rethinking subaltern urbanism. *International Journal of Urban and Regional Research*, 35(2), 223–38. doi:10.1111/j.1468-2427.2011.01051.x

Shatkin, G. (2002). Working with the community: dilemmas in radical planning in Metro Manila, the Philippines. *Planning Theory & Practice*, 3(3), 301–17.

Singh, B. and M. Parmar (2017). Unravelling redevelopment in the megacity context of India. In U. Sengupta and A. Shaw (eds.), *Trends and Issues in Housing in Asia: Coming of an Age*. New Delhi: Routledge.

Singh, B. and M. Sethi (2018). *The Divided City*. Singapore: World Scientific Publishing.

Stecko S. and N Barber. (2007). *Exposing Vulnerabilities: Monsoon Floods Case study prepared for Revisiting Urban Planning: Global Report on Human Settlements*. Available from: http://www.mcgm.gov.in/irj/portal/

Online source

http://smartcity.eletsonline.com/mohua-launched-lap-and-tps-for-25-smart-cities/ accessed on 20 August 2018.

6

CONCLUSION

The current narrative of smart cities in India seems to be a telling tale on greater fragmentation of urban space and governance, superimposition of new systems, introduction of a new lexicon and tech-driven city utopias not completely in sync with the organic and historic realities of urban India. There is time for course correction if we pause and reflect on the current trajectory and factor in crucial components that have been ignored. In this concluding chapter, we pose the same questions that we asked at the very outset: What is the Smart City Mission in India? Is it a paradigm, a laboratory, or a trajectory?

The Smart City Mission (SCM) offers a paradigm shift essentially of technology-driven city utopias and imaginations that override the (in)discipline and messiness of existing cities. The deployment of technologies like artificial intelligence (AI), Internet of Things (IoT), robotics, and Big Data envision the building of smart cities that are governed on the foundation of data constantly collected and run on data-driven systems. In the Union budget of 2018, the SCM aims to build 100 smart cities with state-of-the-art amenities like smart command-and-control centers, solar rooftops, intelligent transport with a focus on automation, quantum communication, IT, machine learning, AI, and robotics. Technology is aimed at creating economic opportunities, enabling transparency in governance, instituting better delivery systems and better and smarter urban spaces – the ultimate goals of the SCM. India is fast emerging as the global hub of IT and IT-enabled services. According to the International Data Corporation, a market research firm, India accounts for 10% of global smart phone sales. The App Annie 2016 Retrospective Report states how in recent years India has surpassed the United States as the second largest smart phone market while also sharply outpacing the United States in the mobile app market (Sinha, 2018b). India is increasingly seen as a growing security and surveillance market with varied government departments like the police and traffic management agencies increasingly adopting innovative technologies mainly supplied by global companies. It is true that technology – especially digital technologies – have significantly altered India's urban story in many ways. Yet tech-driven city utopias like the current smart city narrative pose serious challenges, leave unaddressed gaps, and open new arenas of vulnerabilities and risks.

The SCM in India opens a Pandora's box of many unanswered questions, unaddressed issues, and contradictions. For instance, standardization and uniform norms are not being put in place in sectors like ongoing metro rail projects across the cities of India. E. Sreedharan, former Delhi metro chief, remarked:

> In Russia and Eastern Europe, every metro has the same standards, the same signalling system and track gauge etc. But in India each metro project is importing its own components from different sources, leading to cost escalation. Standardization will reduce costs. Also, once standards are set, you can get things manufactured locally.
>
> *(Dasgupta, 2018)*

Whereas standardization is absent in sectors like metro rail projects, uniform standards, performance benchmarks, and indexes that rank diverse cities with heterogeneous conditions along similar parameters are considered priorities. For instance, the Ease of Living Index that ranked cities on 15 parameters released in 2018 uses issuance of construction permits to rank cities on economy and employment. This could work as a desirable parameter for a new urban center like Amravati, but is it workable for old Delhi or old Kolkata? The contradiction is evident in the SCM narrative that stresses that each city must capitalize on its strengths and build on its uniqueness, while at same time subjecting them to immense competition based on centrally determined parameters. Cities in fact face a paradox; they must remain unique yet respond to the all-pervasive, neoliberal, tech-driven dictates of urbanization. This paradox leads one to rethink the very meaning of smartness and the future pathways of urban India.

The SCM is a trajectory of private capital–led, neoliberal urbanization. This in turn promotes an urbanism of impersonalized spaces symbolized by the rapid rupture of the urban fabric in inner cities and the disconnect from the larger region, with escalating impacts on long-term goals of urban inclusion and urban sustainability. All nation-states, including India, are committed to the Sustainable Development Goals (SDGs) that call for the building of resilient, safe, sustainable, and inclusive cities. These goals mandate that we rethink and reflect on our current urbanization processes.

The SCM in India is a trajectory with misplaced priorities, sometimes lopsided, often ignoring urbanization trends and quintessential features of Indian urbanism like informality, crucial components of urban form and their interrelationships, and cultural and social practices of people and communities. For instance, urban transport tops the list that has received maximum funds under the SCM, while other urban sectors like solid waste management (SWM) have startling low priority. Perhaps this is because SWM is covered under other ongoing programs like the ODF, SBM, and AMRUT. In a situation where the convergence of various urban programs is top priority, even after three years of implementation, many cities have performed abysmally low in the performance benchmarks and indicators set by the government. Misplaced priorities are visible in investment patterns; for instance, beautification of riverfronts has received more priority, with not much attention to the cleaning of rivers. The continuous filth, debris, and sewage pose serious health hazards to the residents living in adjoining areas. The Gomti riverfront project was launched in 2013 with an investment of 1,000 crore that aimed to beautify its banks, channelize the river, and provide other tourist attractions like jogging and cycling tracks, a musical fountain, water theater, and water bus facility (HT Correspondent, 2018b). In a recent initiative the Lucknow municipal corporation has deployed all its 8,000 workers – both on rolls and contractual – in what is known as the Clean Gomti drive. Gomti is a groundwater-fed river that is the cultural mainstay of Lucknow, yet an estimated 27 drains carry sewage waste into the river. Many of these drains are not linked with the main catchment drain that channels through sewer treatment plants. Apart from biodegradable waste, an estimated 10 metric tons of solid waste like construction materials, household waste, and plastic have choked the river (Kumar, 2018a).

Eventually the SCM reduces cities to laboratories for sporadic experiments, usually with technologies supplied by global giants, discussed in Section 1. The growing significance of digital technologies usually controlled by global companies and tech giants have serious implications on citizens' right to privacy, which is now a fundamental right conferred by the Constitution of India, questions of security, and protection discussed in Section 2. The draft bill for data protection 2018 is the first step that address these concerns, but it is still being discussed and debated. Section 3 highlights the institutional challenges resulting from the emergence of new institutions that ultimately spill over and duplicate functions, making urban governance a fuzzy, chaotic terrain. The question of accountability remains a serious concern. Sections 4, 5, and 6 discuss the challenges to smartness posed by the organic character of Indian urbanism and the crucial connections between people, enterprises, and their sociocultural practices that are ignored in this narrative.

Section 1: cities as laboratories

The SCM in India envisions cities and urban sectors that deploy technologies usually available with private companies and global firms. For instance, Egis is a large engineering firm based in France that is working on airport projects in Pune, Lucknow, and Trichy. The company is also aiming to bid for more projects, as the government of India has already announced 50 more airports to be operational in the near future. This global firm is also the program management consultant for smart city projects in Bhubaneshwar and Chandigarh. Apart from that, the company is involved in metro rail projects across cities like Kochi, Chennai, Nagpur, Kolkata, Jaipur, and Pune (Jachiet, 2018, p. 48). The SCM narrative heavily focuses on sectors like urban mobility. In a document titled *National Strategy for Artificial Intelligence#AIFORALL*, released in June 2018, NitiAyog has identified smart cities and smart mobility as two of the areas of focus for AI intervention with zero emission vehicles as top priority (http:// niti.gov.in/writereaddata/files/document_publication/NationalStrategy-for-AI-Discussion-Paper.pdf). Smart cities driven by new technologies aim to create new economic and employment opportunities for youth. Startups, tech enterprises, and digital solutions are the new buzzwords. In a bid to involve citizens and create opportunities for youth, NitiAyog recently launched a tech platform called MoveHack (http://niti.gov.in/), a global mobility hackathon inviting solutions, prototypes, and ideas to address issues of mobility and transportation in India with a cash prize of over Rs 2 crore.

Experiments are underway, especially in sectors like traffic management and police, adopting the latest technologies and applications like never before. Security, safety, and surveillance are the new lexicon used to enable better performance of these sectors. This is turn is envisioned to translate into smarter cities. For example, technologies like automatic number plate recognition (ANPR) can automate the process of traffic management and book vehicles that violate traffic, rules along with video proof. Intelligent digital sensors like bionic ears can help in policing. There is heavy deployment of technologies in the urban mobility sector, yet there is hardly any thought for simple urban design interventions like wider sidewalks; safe streets for women, children, senior citizens, and differently abled people; and last-mile connectivity.

There is widespread introduction of expensive technologies even in areas where low-cost methods and common practices would suffice. For instance, in the SWM sector, a lot can be achieved only if we emphasize segregation at the source. In a recent article, "Expensive technologies can't solve waste problem" in the *Hindustan Times*, Manshi Asher, an environment researcher from Himachal Pradesh, notes:

> According to the World Bank, the country's daily waste generation will reach 377,000 tonnes by 2025. To tackle this challenge, several Indian municipalities have invested in smart bins. The smart bins are different from the usual bins: they have twin underground chambers (one for biodegradable and another for non-biodegradable waste) and are fitted with sensors which send out alerts when a bin is about to get full. The cost of procurement and installation of one bin is between 4 to 8.5 lakhs and a

special crane mounted truck which pulls out the bins from the chambers and carries them to a landfill is between 50 and 55 lakhs. They don't contribute much as they don't segregate waste at source so having two bins don't serve any purpose as users and collectors dump mixed waste in them.

She adds that for any recycling, sorting, and segregation, human handling is a must, and this is done by waste collectors. But smart bins eliminate the possibility of human intervention at the site, thereby also adversely affecting the livelihood of the waste picker community. From the experience of Dharmashala, which was listed as a smart city in 2016, Asher explains how the smart bin experience was marred in the first month after a few of the underground concrete structures caved in due to the hilly terrain and lack of consideration for underground drainage in an area that sees heavy rainfall. In a city that has only one disposal site and has yet to plan the setting up of a waste processing unit, it makes little sense to spend crores on the new bins. She adds that it is also an oversight of the SWM Rules of 2016, which require segregation, processing, and recycling of waste. The rules hold urban local bodies (ULBs) and users at the source responsible for managing the waste. Policymakers should instead focus on simple measures: segregation at the source, processing, organizing, and capacity building of citizens and waste handlers (Asher, 2018).

Section 2: smart technologies, citizens' rights, privacy, and security

It is evident from the discussion that SCM envisions cities that are technology driven with the underlying understanding that efficient surveillance and monitoring systems are the best ways to govern cities. First, the implementation of such systems depends on the collection of huge amounts of data – even citizens' personal data – at the disposal of government institutions, global tech giants, and private firms. The use of the latest technologies like locational data and algorithms to understand citizen-consumer behavior and preferences and to monitor them has serious implications on the questions of right to privacy, security, and safety of citizens. The draft Data Protection bill is the first step to address these concerns.

Second, too much dependency on technologies carries attendant risks and vulnerabilities. Cybersecurity is a matter of grave concern. A report by Cyber Security Ventures predicts that global annual cyber-crime costs will grow to $6 trillion by 2021, which includes destruction and theft of data and intellectual property, stolen money, fraud, and damage of infrastructure data. Hackers can tamper with traffic control systems, smart street lighting, city management systems that control orders and other facilities, public transport, smart grids, wireless sensors that control waste and water management, and mobile and cloud networks (Shukla, 2017).

Finally, the SCM narrative is built on this central philosophy. Safety and security necessitate surveillance, the Foucauldian idea of a Panopticon. Recently, a social media hub to monitor the exchanges of citizens was mooted. The social media hub was suggested as a response to the rumors spread by social media messages that spread mass violence and unrest. The widespread use of social media has its own perils and security concerns, and surveillance seems to be the only response to these growing concerns. In the end, the crucial questions of accountability and control remain. The narrative also threatens to break the social contract between citizens and state institutions; instils a culture of distrust, fear, and anxiety; and misses the crucial humane stance.

Cities are increasingly at risk of losing vital connections between people and places, character and fabric, as order is sought to be maintained not by eyes on the street but by closed-circuit television (CCTV) cameras. This paradox leads one to actually rethink the very meaning of smartness and what kind of cities we want for ourselves. Maimunah Mohd Sharif, the first Asian woman to serve as executive director of the United Nations Human Settlements Program (UN-Habitat), remarks:

> I think it's the human aspect that's sometimes lacking. For example, in urban planning, we talk about safe cities. To do this, we often put up CCTV, all the technology. But actually, you can create a safe city through design if you are humane enough – if you think hard about human nature and human needs.
>
> *(www.oxfordurbanists.com/magazine/2018/6/25/*
> *un-habitat-director-ms-maimunah-mohd-sharif)*

In an interesting article, Vivek Wadhwa, Distinguished Fellow at Harvard Law School, states, "[T]ackling today's social and technological challenges requires the ability to think critically about the human context, something that Humanities graduates happen to be best trained to be." In the same article he gives examples of Silicon Valley's brightest stars who aren't engineers but liberal arts and humanities majors. These include LinkedIn's founder Reid Hoffman, who has a master's in philosophy; YouTube's CEO, Susan Wojcicki, who majored in history and literature; and Chinese tech firm Alibaba's CEO Jack Ma, who has a BA in English. Wadhwa explains that an engineering degree is valuable, but the sense of empathy that comes from music, arts, literature, and psychology provides a big advantage in design. A history major who has studied the Enlightenment or the rise and fall of the Roman Empire gains an insight into the human elements of technology and the importance of its usability. A psychologist is more likely to know how to motivate people and to understand what users want than is an engineer who has worked only in the technology trenches. He adds that a musician or artist is king in a world in which you can 3D print anything that you can imagine (Wadhwa, 2018).

Section 3: institutional challenges to smartness

Capacity building of local institutions, like the municipal authorities, has been a mandate since the enforcement of the 74th Constitutional Amendment Act in 1992. Municipal authorities, including corporations, councils, and *nagar panchayats*, suffer from lack of human and sometimes financial resources, inefficiency, and sluggishness. The mandatory city functions still remain the constitutional duties of the municipal authorities in our cities, yet not much has been done to increase the capacity of these basic institutions. Besides, the widespread use of IT and digital technologies in the day-to-day functioning of governance requires training of the existing staff.

A special-purpose vehicle (SPV) will be a nodal agency in implementing this program. It will plan, appraise, approve, release funds, implement, manage, operate, monitor, and evaluate the smart city development projects. The SPV in turn appoints project management consultants (PMCs) for designing, developing, managing, and implementing area-based projects. SPVs may take assistance from any of the empaneled consulting firms in the list prepared by the MoUD and the handholding agencies. For the procurement of goods and services, transparent and fair procedures as prescribed under the state/ULB financial rules may be followed. Vesting planning, appraisal, approval, release of funds, and overall management of projects in the hands of an SPV as proposed in Smart City Plans further undermine the powers and capacities of the third tier of governance (i.e. the municipalities). With so many agencies involved in the implementation, the question of accountability always remains. In a situation where the municipal authority is not adequately capable, this poses a bigger challenge. Vesting all powers of urban management to centrally appointed bureaucrats manning SPVs raises questions of democratic, transparent, and equitable governance. In this scenario, the elected representatives at the city level are completely disempowered, while international firms decide the destiny of cities.

The entry and presence of several institutions and agencies, including international ones, has been a growing trend in urban governance in India since the late 1990s. The urban sector in India has been a melting point of several policies and programs since then. Besides, institutional innovations like public–private partnerships and outsourcing of services have been in vogue with varied outcomes. Institutions also traverse the areas of informal networks and politics that have significant impacts on decision making and outcomes. The SCM is characterized by rampant privatization; low accountability; increasing vulnerabilities of large sections of citizens; and a set of benchmarks, rankings, indicators, and checklists that encourages fierce competition among cities and states for central funds and desperate attempts to entice private investments.

Emerging peri-urban areas with ambiguous civic statuses pose serious institutional challenges to smart urbanism, with serious implications on sustainability and equity. Cities across India are increasingly experiencing peri-urban growth where rural and urban features tend to coexist on the periphery and beyond their limits. This often creates confusion on demarcating a territory as *panchayat, nagar panchayat*, municipal council, or municipal corporation. Despite available definitions and set criteria, the existing features of these areas often pose major challenges to acquiring the appropriate civic status. It has been observed that many of these peri-urban areas that have recently sprung up near big cities suffer from official apathy with no attendant services like water supply, sanitation, garbage collection and disposal, street cleaning, and lighting, as they have not been given urban civic status. Often, these services are privately provided, thereby increasing the living expenses in these areas. Without any governance mechanism, these areas are also subject to environmental vulnerabilities. The lack of supporting physical infrastructure like roads, modes of public transport, and social infrastructure, such as schools, colleges, hospitals, and cultural and recreational centers, are major concerns for people living and migrating to peri-urban areas.

Section 4: challenges of equity and sustainability to smartness

The processes of peri-urbanization compel newly formed, often unequal and stark, connections with adjoining rural belts. It's not unusual to stumble upon huge swathes of open fields, unoccupied or under-construction sites adjacent to swanky residential and commercial enclaves. The forced and often unequal and stark (dis)connects with adjoining rural belts create environmental imbalances. The emerging new towns, smart cities, and city extensions represent what is often termed a *bypass urbanization* that eats away at ecological commons like wetlands, mangroves, saltpans, forests, and water reserves that are crucial for economic production, for providing livelihoods to varied communities, and for the ecological sustainability of the larger adjoining region (for details see Allen, 2009; Shaw, 2005; Baviskar, 2003, 2011; D'Souza and Nagendra, 2011; Bose, 2013; Marotta, 2014). Growing demands and economic pressures in turn create environmental imbalance, with the larger regions of the emergent new towns and cities resulting in increased environmental vulnerabilities and climate change risks, particularly for the vulnerable sections like the poor, aged, women and children, and ethnic minorities. Cities can't continue to grow rich at the expense of their rural hinterlands. The peri-urban reality in India compels policymakers, planners, and urban practitioners to step back from treating the city as a stand-alone entity and take a look at the region as a whole. The vital ecological and economic linkages between the urban and the larger region, the upcoming transitional areas awaiting civic status, and the surrounding rural areas have to be seen as a system from a sustainable environmental and equitable perspective. This includes addressing current consumption patterns, cutting short supply chains, growing locally, and bridging the resource gap in order to make the peri-urban reality more inclusive and sustainable.

BOX 6.1: THE DOMINANT TRENDS OF INDIA'S URBANIZATION

India's urbanization story currently unfolds in two dominant patterns: expansion of its suburbs or peri-urban growth and a simultaneous rupture of its inner (often historic) core. The challenges to smartness are tied to the current urbanization process in the country essentially driven by neoliberal logic, private capital, and tech-driven utopias that are silent on issues of equity and sustainability. Peri-urbanization and ribbon development are the dominant patterns in India's urbanization story which favors urban sprawl, intrinsically following the American model of creating suburbs, downtowns, and automobiles to connect them. This is further bolstered by private investments, capital and attendant modes of urban governance that allow such urbanization at a faster pace. With liberalization and the onslaught of global forces, most cities have witnessed a real estate boom and the entry of private players. A series of urban development projects ranging from residential and commercial complexes and physical infrastructure like roads and flyovers rolled out in the decades after the 1990s. This pattern of urbanization, often termed bypass strategy, characterized by peri-urban growth continues today, with not much focus on urban regeneration strategies. It is not surprising that the contemporary city in India is a city of contrasts with marked distinctions between old and new territories.

The peri-urban reality is depicted in upcoming commercial and residential townships, smart cities, new towns, city extensions, infrastructure projects, transportation corridors, and special economic zones – all of which open up new challenges to the questions of urban governance and environmental sustainability. The visible spatial transformations are particularly witnessed in the form of high-rise buildings and gated communities mushrooming in the peripheries of gradually expanding city limits. Often, life remains confined within the self-sustaining gated community. Outside the gates, sparse interactions of people, communities, and mobilities fail to create the much-needed social interconnections that constitute urban life. It is not surprising that with such huge tracts of land, under-construction sites, unoccupied buildings, fast-moving vehicles in adjoining highways, and lack of dense social life, peri-urban areas become havens for crimes, especially against women and children.

Socioeconomic forces are creating new demands for real estate, commercial, residential, and leisure spaces, which in turn call for densification and horizontal expansion of the city. One cannot miss the rampant usage of international names and imagery of the newly emerging high-end apartments dotting the peripheral expansion of cities like Kolkata, Surat, and Lucknow, confirming their global aspirations. These new imageries and structures often seem as sudden jerks to the people driving through, creating sharp visual divisions with the surrounding rural landscape. It is perhaps easier to identify peri-urban areas by features and processes than to look at fixed geographical distances or boundaries. These areas are transitional in character with intense land use change, contested natural resource use, rapid migration, and emerging lifestyles that often replace pre-existing modes of urbanism. The peri-urban reality of India throws new challenges that require new ways of looking at the rural and urban not as divides anymore, but as a continuum. The SCM is silent on the larger trends of urbanization and how it envisions to address the challenges they pose.

Although greenfield developments, new towns, and select city extensions seem to be some of the common features in India's urbanization pattern, so are dilapidation, blight, and the rupture of inner-city areas. This division is starkly visible in the architectural and visual divide and in the segregation of communities, whereby the poor continue to inhabit the dilapidated zones, while the rich move out to the newer areas. As a result, the city core remains neglected with no attendant policy on conservation or regeneration. The forlorn, dilapidated tale of inner cities located in the older parts of many Indian cities is best depicted through films and literature but seldom grabs the attention of policymakers. The overcrowded inner cities of India represent the organic growth, diversity, and dense social life that one encounters in locations like the *Shobhabazaar* in Kolkata, *Chowk* in Lucknow, and *Nai Sadak* in Delhi. The inner cities of India like Chowk in Lucknow represent the organic character that is in danger of rapid dilution. We have already witnessed that many parts of Chowk are changing fast. The now-dilapidated spaces that qualify as living heritage are testimonies of the history and culture of our glorious cities. The place-specific cultural identity of our inner cities appeals to the romantic tourist and the enthusiastic traveler. Cities could do a lot better by conserving the run-down inner areas and rethinking and revaluating their current policy. For instance, in Lucknow, area-based development currently underway in the Smart Cities Plan only focuses on a small area demarcated for conservation in Qaiserbagh. The larger inner core of Chowk with its bustling social life reflected in the presence of innumerable arts and crafts and practicing craftsmen still living and working in those areas are simply forgotten. We have yet to come across a plan or strategy or vision document from any government agency in Lucknow that has put in some thought to reviving the lost cultural and historical glory of Chowk, which stands for everything that Lucknow city represents. The conservation efforts must include restoring the original character of the historic core. Such a holistic approach requires reviving traditional occupations and enhancing the economic conditions, like those of the weavers. This in turn will revive the living and working spaces, like those of the weavers' colony and artists' lanes, and prevent further migration. The SCM is looking into core area. The inner core area of Lucknow is actually Chowk. It is a difficult space to handle, with multiple issues that need immediate redressal. When the heritage zone was being identified, it included many important places like Residency, Chowk tower, various monuments, Qaiserbagh, and many others. But surprisingly Chowk was left out. Chowk has always been a neglected spatiality. Even heritage boundaries identified earlier did not include it. That neglect is carried on in the current SCM as well. Under the SCM only 60 acres in Qaiserbagh are identified under the area-based development plan with retrofitting solutions. It's easy to handle and has open spaces and builds on the previous 2010 plan.

Section 5: people, enterprises, sociocultural practices, and challenges to smartness

The inner cores of second-tier historic cities in India discussed in this volume that are now designated for smart city experiments are characterized by displacement of communities and loss of urban fabric. For instance, in the inner-city locations of Lucknow, like Hussainabad, Aminadabad, and Chowk, a few renowned, old, wealthy families have managed to retain their ancestral homes and eke out a living from their traditional professions in inner cities. With changing times, the devalorization of traditional occupations and lack of social infrastructure like schools and colleges, most of the older residents have either migrated to newer upcoming areas in search of better economic prospects or relocated to adjoining bigger cities. The communities left behind are mostly occupied in petty businesses, like running small shops or street vending, and live and work under abysmal conditions.

Further, culture and creative industries based on immaterial labor are increasingly replacing other forms of work characteristic of erstwhile industrial, manufacturing-based societies. The dispersed and flexible nature of production has actually changed the way cities function, with a wide range of employment opportunities in the production of entertainment, advertising, fashion, tourism, hospitality industry, finance, banking and insurance, academia, research and development, information, and communication. Second-tier historic cities like Varanasi, Lucknow, and Jaipur discussed as case studies in this volume could leverage on their cultural capital, rethink ways and means of engaging local communities that are adept in local arts and crafts in newly emerging creative industries while maintaining the urban form.

Culture- and heritage-based development always calls for an integrated approach linking local, often poor, communities, basic services, and infrastructure with a corresponding rise in tourism. When these components are integrated through a set of carefully laid out plans and strategies using the knowledge and skill sets of the locals, real development is possible. The recent attack on foreign tourists in *Fatehpur Sikri* near Agra (handiwork of unemployed locals called *lapkas*) raises important questions on the missing links and gaps that need to be addressed urgently. For one, integrating the local community by first mapping their skill sets; determining the presence of creative industries (if any); assessing the possibilities of livelihoods; and improving their habitats via connecting roads and basic services like water, sewage, and waste disposal can go a long way to what we now understand as pro-poor tourism, the need of the hour. This assumes even more significance for cities like Jaipur and Agra, whose economies thrive on tourism. Merely calculating tourist numbers is not enough. Smart cities capitalizing on tourism can do a lot better from global learnings that have successfully built revenue models by integrating planning and development of entire cities around heritage structures.

BOX 6.2: A NOTE ON URBANITY

Urbanity results from culture as practiced through the everyday urbanism of interactions between people and place. This term is usually understood as characterized with diversity, physically through mixed-use development strategy, and sociologically through the cultural matrix that enhances the quality of urban existence. It brings together strands of thought from urban design and planning, like those of Jane Jacobs (1961), Kevin Lynch (1984), John Montgomery (1998), and John Friedmann (2010), who associate diversity with the existence of multiple lifestyles, cultural innovations, contestations, and conflict rather than uniformity, stability, or order. Thus, density, mixed use, cultural heterogeneity, and permeability are the crucial components of urbanity that make urban spaces livable and attractive. The concept of urbanity also draws from the classical works of urban sociologists like Georg Simmel and Louis Wirth, who interpret urbanity as a way of life, interwoven with human relations and characterized by three essential features of scale, density, and heterogeneity. Urban designers and planners emphasize the legitimate role of physical design strategies to foster urbanity, while urban sociologists underscore the importance of cultural, social, and economic drivers. It is this organic, spontaneous, unexpected, sometimes messy, and chaotic quality brought about with the interactions of places and people that makes up the urban experience and helps in providing place-based character to the city. Performed repeatedly, these reiterative social practices render the city as a theater of social life, as claimed by Simmel many years ago, and maintain safety and social order through what Jacobs describes as eyes on the street. The crucial element is activity

> that can glue physical, social, and psychological dimensions together and that produce and mirror quality in the built environment. As Montgomery points out, "successful places are a combination of three elements: spaces, activities and people" (Montgomery, 1998). In this sense, the intensity and diversity of activities can be seen as a determinant indicator to measure urban quality.

Section 6: Indian urbanism and challenges to smartness

The oft-neglected and forgotten narrow *gullies, mohallas,* neighborhoods, lanes, and by-lanes are valuable because they help preserve the urban fabric – the fundamental character and identity of the city. They also add value as the smallest social spheres of urban life, cherished and celebrated by people, acting as public space by virtue of their inclusiveness, and maintaining informalized forms of social order.

The social and cultural homogeneity of inner cities is transforming with erstwhile traditional occupations and enterprises fast vanishing, together with the displacement of communities practicing those occupations. For instance, some parts of Chowk in old Lucknow are fast changing, and many of its *old gullies* have come to be lined with fast food stalls selling Chinese and Italian dishes replacing traditional snacks. The rhythmic sounds of hammering produced by craftsmen busy with *warq ka kaam* are replaced with the glaring loud noise of moving traffic. The *Unani dawakhana* houses designer boutiques selling exclusive *chikankari* and *zardozi* embroidered garments. The solitary presence of a *hakim sahib* reminds us of the original use of this place. All the rest has been encroached upon and put to varied uses: grocery shops, coaching centers, beauty parlors, and new houses, possibly with new residents.

Gentrification as a social/urban policy has been widely used in the United States, UK, and Netherlands. Usually it means redevelopment of inner-city housing stock in order to entice middle-income groups to blighted neighborhoods. This is believed to lead to positive effects in terms of revitalizing run-down inner-city areas that would result in generating employment opportunities for the poor already residing there and a rise in real estate stock and property prices, widening the fiscal base of local governments. Usually terms like urban revitalization or urban renaissance (as in the UK) and urban regeneration have been used in the deployment of this urban policy in Northern cities. Gentrification works in a piecemeal way in Indian cities because of the strong presence of informal settlements that are difficult to displace.

Job creation in the informal sector could be possible with city-level planning. However, so far there is not much clarity about economic activities in a city, whereas ideally the planning for cities should be done keeping its economic activities in mind. Approximately 50% of people in the informal sector – like street vendors, laborers, food vendors, and rag pickers – are not being absorbed by the city. Keeping in mind that the city management is most important for an individual's growth, there is a need to revamp the way planning is done. Structural reforms are required to add these informal-sector employees/employment creators into the urban plans. Some amount of judicial intervention and civil society activism might help in this process.

In a very significant judgment, the Supreme Court ruled that, if properly regulated according to the exigency of the circumstances, the small traders on the sidewalks could considerably add to the comfort and convenience of the general public by making available ordinary articles of everyday use for a comparatively lesser price. An ordinary person, not very affluent, while hurrying towards his home after a day's work can pick up these articles without going out of his way to find a regular market. The right to carry on trade or business mentioned in Article 19(1)g of the constitution of India on street pavements, if properly regulated, cannot be denied on the grounds that the streets are meant exclusively for passing or repassing and no other use (*Sodhan Singh* v. NDMC, 1989). This Supreme Court ruling is significant, because it emphasizes several important aspects of street vending and the use of public space. The judgment notes that street vending, if regulated, cannot be denied merely on the grounds that pavements are meant exclusively for pedestrians. The most important aspect is that street vendors are exercising their constitutional right to carry out trade or business; hence, it should be regulated properly and not abolished.

Section 7: conclusion

The Smart City paradigm, along with a spate of urban policies like AMRUT, ODF, and Digital India, has laid out the future pathways of urban India. Many of these initiatives are carried forward from earlier regimes, like the JNNURM, but set forth with new rigor and competitiveness. City governments are too stressed over the performance benchmarks, which often remain as mere checklists. In addition, cities are fiercely competing for central funds. In this fervor, the fundamental questions of accountability; citizens' right to privacy, safety, and security; traditional occupations and enterprises; loss of urban fabric; social displacement; disconnects between people and places; and disconnects between new cities and adjoining regions are left unanswered. A shift in thinking from technology-driven solutions to people-centric solutions could help us work towards more inclusive and sustainable smart cities. Smart cities are about smart people and creating opportunities for people with the help of new technologies. The opportunities must not be limited to coming up with solutions and technologies only, but must address how these technologies could in turn create new economic opportunities, especially for those in lower socioeconomic brackets.

A humane approach to smartness that is simultaneously culturally and socially responsive, environmentally sustainable, and equitable will complete this quest to smartness. Urban programs like SBM and ODF could not meet their targets because communities have not adopted them on a large scale. Many cities could not build adequate toilets. Even in situations where toilets were constructed and accessible, cultural practices and age-old traditions prevent people from using them. Poor maintenance, lack of water, and nonfunctional doorknobs and taps are other reasons for programs like SBM and ODF not reaching their logical outcomes.

The future urban pathways lie in the local diversity of cities in the face of a universal model of globalization, neoliberal capitalism, and technologically driven urban utopias. Local diversity demonstrates a much more complex microcosm, which renders the contemporary city as a place of constant vibrancy, innovation, and social change. The sociocultural diversity and its spatial implications have economic and practical bases too, which influence it and in turn get affected. The global character of India's cities is not restricted to high-end malls, real estate markets, posh residential complexes, and IT parks, but also informal economies in slums of Dharavi in Mumbai and weavers; colonies in dilapidated Chowk of Lucknow and several such settlements that cater to global supply chains. It is therefore difficult to find a Western model of gentrification of metropolises in India. Unlike in European cities or the one-off case of mill lands in Mumbai, the strategy of gentrification has not worked in India's historical cores, be it Lucknow, Jaipur, Agra, Madurai, Mysore, or any other second-tier historic city. This is because of the presence of a large informal economy and the continued presence of varied social groups engaged in petty trades and jobs catering to supply chains that have both local and global economic linkages. This essentially indicates that in order to promote social and spatial diversity in cities, the traditional practices of designing, building and sustaining them have to be prioritized. Theoretical ideas of creating a good urban place with community/neighborhood-level planning especially focusing on informal settlements have been suggested in this volume. The reintroduction of the LAP in select 25 smart cities announced by the government of India (GoI) in June 2018 is a welcome move. There's an imminent need to rethink current modes of planning and look for better approaches, alternative visions, and connect people and communities that address the long-term goals of inclusion and sustainability tied to the global urban discourse on SDGs and the New Urban Agenda.

BOX 6.3: MAPPING OF CREATIVE INDUSTRIES AND EMPLOYMENT GENERATION

In a ground-breaking ceremony, the One District One Product summit was inaugurated in Lucknow on 29 July 2018 with the aim to make Uttar Pradesh (UP) a trillion-dollar economy in the near future by boosting its micro and small industries. The main focus of the summit was to brand UP's unique products, culture, and creative industries in the national and international markets that would in turn generate employment opportunities and arrest migration to metros. In a two-day event artisans from all over the state displayed their artefacts at 268 stalls. These included famous products like carpets of Bhadohi, brassware of Moradabad, locks of Aligarh, black pottery of Mirzapur, crockery of Khurja, leather of Agra and Kanpur, Chikankar textiles of Lucknow, wooden toys of Varanasi, and flutes of Pilibhit, among others. The state government of UP also signed five 5 MoUs, including one with the e-commerce giant Amazon India, to promote products selected under the One District One Product scheme at the summit. Other announcements made at the summit include the establishment of common facility centers, testing labs, and design studios to enable artisans to work and improve their products; Rs 1,006.94 crore loans to 4,095 artisans across the state; and an ambitious project "Vishwakarma Shram Samman", for artisans (HT Correspondent, 2018a). The summit also selected special food items from 11 districts of UP, like pulses from Gonda and Balrampur, rice from Siddharthnagar, guava from Allahabad, gooseberry from Pratapgarh, banana from Koshambi, and potatoes from Etawah. The summit mooted the idea of boosting exports from UP. It was proposed that organizations like the Agricultural and Processes Food Products Export Development Authority (APEDA) can help promote local food items in national and international markets – setting up mega and mini food parks – and develop elaborate business plans, pick one famous food product from each district, and help in setting up food processing industries and creating local employment opportunities (Singh, 2018a).

At the event's conclusion, veteran fashion designer Varija Baja proposed that the UP government can generate employment for its youth by combining fashion, film, and tourism. The idea of how Khadi can be promoted at the Kumbh Mela was also mooted. The idea of aggressive promotion of the state's crafts like the Banarasi saree, zardozi, and chikankari also was discussed (Mix of fashion, film and tourism can do wonders: Varija Bajaj in My City, 2018). Communities engaged in traditional occupations like perfume making and saree and carpet making indigenously manufactured in many second-tier historic cities are adapting to new technologies and digital platforms to survive in changing times.

Online food aggregators like Zomato and Swiggy partner with local food stalls capitalizing on local flavors and promoting them aggressively. Such online services serve as great connections between consumers who get local delicacies served at their doorstep and local food vendors who were on the verge of closing down but now get help promoting their business (Kumar, 2018b).

References

Allen, A. (2009). Sustainable cities or sustainable urbanisation. *Palette UCL's Journal of Sustainable Cities*, 1(2).

Asher, M. (2018). Expensive technologies can't solve waste problem in the Hindustan Times. *Hindustan Times*, Lucknow, 26 July, p. 10.

Baviskar, A. (2003). Between violence and desire: space, power, and identity in the making of metropolitan Delhi. *International Social Science Journal*, 55(175), 89–98.

Baviskar, A. (2011). Cows, cars and cycle-rickshaws: Bourgeois environmentalism and the battle for Delhi's streets. in A Baviskar and R. Ray (eds.). Elite and Everyman: The Cultural Politics of the Indian Middle Classes. New Delhi: Routledge.

Bose, P. (2013). Bourgeois environmentalism, leftist development and neoliberal urbanism in the city of joy. In T. S. Samara, H. Shenjing, and C. Guo (eds.), *Locating Right to the City in the Global South*. Abingdon and New York: Routledge.

Dasgupta, M. (2018). All metro systems to have standard norms nationwide. *Hindustan Times*, Lucknow edition, 25 June, p. 1.

D'Souza, R. and H. Nagendra (2011). Changes in public commons as a consequence of urbanization: the Agara Lake in Bangalore, India. *Environmental Management*, 47(5), 840–50.

Friedmann, J. (2010). Place and place-making in cities: a global perspective. *Planning Theory & Practice*, 11(2), 149–65.

HT Correspondent (2018a). Branding must to make UP trillion $economy. *Hindustan Times*, Lucknow, Saturday 11 August, p. 5.

HT Correspondent (2018b). Riverfront facelift to be completed by Diwali. *Hindustan Times*, Lucknow, 18 July, p. 3.

Jachiet, N. (2018). As a French Company Sustainability is something that we live by, Interview with Nicolas Jachiet, Chairman and CEO Egis Group, BW Smart Cities World, April–May 2018, p. 48. *bwsmartcities.businessworld*. Retrieved from http://bwsmartcities.businessworld.in/article/-As-a-French-company-sustainability-is-something-that-we-live-by-/06-07-2018-154094/

Jacobs, J. (1961). *The Death and Life of Great American Cities*. New York: Vintage Books.

Kumar, C. (2018a). Untreated sewage killing our lifeline. *HT Lucknow Hindustan Times*, Lucknow edition, Monday 9 July 2018, p. 2.

Kumar, C. (2018b). Online food delivery gets hotter. *Hindustan Times*, Lucknow, 5 August 2018, p. 3.

Lynch, K. (1984). *Good City Form*. Cambridge, MA: MIT Press.

Marotta, S. (2014) On the critical relationship between citizenship and governance: the case of water management in Italy. *Urbanities*, 4(2), 39–50. www.anthrojournal-urbanities.com/vol-4-no-2-november-2014/ accessed on 10 June 2019.

Mix of fashion, film and tourism can do wonders: Varija Bajaj in My City (2018). *Hindustan Times*, Lucknow, Wednesday 15 August, p. 3.

Montgomery, J. (1998). Making a city: urbanity, vitality and urban design. *Journal of Urban Design*, 3(1), 93–116.

Shaw, A. (2005). Peri-urban interface of Indian cities: growth, governance and local initiatives. *Economic & Political Weekly*, 40(2), 129–36.

Shukla, A. (2017). Smart or not, everyone wants a safe city. *BW Smart Cities World*, November–December, p. 21.

Singh, P. (2018a). Now food products on state ODOP list, specialties from 11 districts identified. *The Times of India*, Lucknow, 11 August, p. 30.

Sinha, P. (2018b). The new age testament-roti Kapra Makaan and internet, guest column. *BW Smart Cities World*, February–March, p. 46.

Sodhan Singh v. NDMC,1989 in Bhowmik, 2003. Bhowmik, S.K. (2003). Urban Responses to Street Trading: India. Research paper. Mumbai: University of Mumbai.

Wadhwa, V. (2018). India needs musicians and artists to work in tandem with engineers. *Hindustan Times*, New Delhi, 23 June, p. 16.

Online sources

http://niti.gov.in/writereaddata/files/document_publication/NationalStrategy-for-AI-Discussion-Paper.pdf accessed on 1 November 2018.

www.oxfordurbanists.com/magazine/2018/6/25/un-habitat-director-ms-maimunah-mohd-sharif accessed on 25 September 2018.

INDEX

Note: Page numbers in *italic* indicate a *figure* and page numbers in **bold** indicate a table on the corresponding page.